PEOPLEWATCHING

Digging Holes and other Adventures

By

Paul Cox

authorHOUSE

1663 Liberty Drive, Suite 200
Bloomington, Indiana 47403
(800) 839-8640
www.authorhouse.com

© *2004 Paul Cox*
All Rights Reserved.

No part of this book may be reproduced, stored in a retrieval system, or transmitted by any means without the written permission of the author.

First published by AuthorHouse 07/16/04

ISBN: 1-4184-7755-9 (sc)

Printed in the United States of America
Bloomington, Indiana

This book is printed on acid-free paper.

Table of Contents

WATCHING PEOPLE 1
    A Trip to the Zoo... 3
    Finding Faces... 5
    Fun At The Movies 7
    A Consumer's Complaint... 9
    A Southerner Remembers Heat 11
    Buying Clothes.. 13
    Spies. Sunlight. Diabetes. Guacamole...................................... 16
    My Wall Companion... 18
    Family Portraits.. 20
    Becoming Bda... 22
    Who's In Charge Here? 24
    What Do You Say to That, Sir?... 26
    Fleshy Things on the Beach.. 28
    Why I Do Not Want Contact Lenses 30
    Watching Watches.. 32

GAMES KIDS AND OTHER PEOPLE PLAY 35
    Games People Could Play If They Wanted To 37
    A Lesson In Flying... 39
    A Verbal Prestige-Enhancement Procedure 41
    Announcing Xtreme Baseball... 44
    A Baseball Story... 47
    Basketball And The Human Condition Explained 49
    Competing By and Over The Rules 51
    Differences in Socksual Perspective.. 53
    Football Practice... 55
    How To Avoid Losing At Poker 57
    How To Be A Little Deaf... 59
    I Know! Let's Go Camping! 61
    The Art Of The Long Game 63
    The Scooter Phenomenon 65
    The Tennis Scoring Mystery Explained At Last.................... 67
    Tough Times 69
    Two Marriage Strategies That Work....................................... 71
    Winning at Conversation 73

LESSONS **75**
    The Lesson of Pinball 77
    The Guy Who Smelled As A Dog 79
    A Lesson About Gardening 81
    Dilemmas Involving Portraits and Ceiling Fans 83
    How Spiders Shout 85
    The Project That Wouldn't Fly 87
    Thoughts on Toast Management and Injustice 90
    Some Thoughts About Stones 93
    What Mosquitoes Mean 95
    Some Thoughts on Peanuts and Order 97

THINGS PEOPLE DO **99**
    Follow Your Dream to Whitney, NE 101
    The Great Yard Sale Adventure 103
    The Red Dodge of Carriage 105
    A Confession Involving The Saxophone 107
    A Mountaintop Experience on a Rooftop 109
    Beam Me Ever Upward, Scotty 112
    Home Maintenance Made Easy 114
    Helping Daddy Around the House 116
    Choosing a Barbershop 118
    How to Speak the Special, Horrific Language of TV 121
    The Mystery of TV Mystery 123
    Your Preview of the New TV Season! (Also the Previous) 125
    The End of the Action-Adventure Era (for Me) 128
    Columnist Explains Other People's Snoring 130
    An Issue of Social Dexterity 132
    Noises in the Night 134
    Pray for the Lights to Go Out 136
    About the Three (or So) Stooges 138
    What Did I Do When I Did It? 140
    WHACK! It's a Blow to the Head! 142
    Selecting a New Car 144
    A Portrait of the Artist as a Young Dud 146
    Living By the Rules 148

LIVING DANGEROUSLY **151**
    Living Dangerously - 1 153
    Living Dangerously - 2 155
    Living Dangerously - 3 157

SONGPIGS, BEARS, SKUNKS 159
   Songpigs of North America 161
   Our Pet Bear 163
   Do Other Animals Have Fun? 165
   Getting To Know The Bear 167
   How Lazy My Cat Is... 169
   Our Wild Life With The Wildlife 171
   Introducing What's Her Name 173
   The Great Plot Against Or Maybe On Behalf Of Humans 175
   Deer and Table Manners 177
   An Update And A Philosophical Query 179

NATURE AND THE SEASONS 181
   What To Do When It's Winter Outdoors 183
   The Return of Spring... 185
   Thoughts On The End of Summer 187
   The Seasons of Beginning 189
   Gardens and Mazes 191
   The Big Bang... 193
   The Bird Club.. 195
   Birds and Bees and Flowers and Us............................... 197

FOOD, SO TO SPEAK 199
   Eggplant and Other Culinary Horrors 201
   Broccoli and the Presidency: An Analysis....................... 203
   A Lesson Involving Peanut Butter 205
   Horrifying Peanut Butter Usages................................... 207
   A Gourmet's Guide to Fine Fast Dining.......................... 209
   The Cookie Issue... 211
   The Cookie Issue – Part II... 213
   Cookie Research Project Continues 215
   The Corn Bread Rules 217
   In Defense of Fruitcake 219
   Let's Hear It for—Corn!... 221
   Important Thoughts About Pizza................................... 223
   The Importance of Potatoes In Western Thought 225
   The Decline And Fall Of Onion Rings............................. 227
   Ordering A Hamburger 229
   The Marmalade Question.. 232
   How To Make Fine Pudding... 234
   A Few Words about Breakfast...................................... 236
   What To Do With A Basket of Crabs............................. 238

MEMORIES **241**
   Digging Holes 243
   How I Spent My Summer Vacation 245
   Summer School The Right Way 247
   A Good, Long Conversation 249
   My Brief and Undistinguished Dancing Career....................251
   Memories: A Small Cemetery in Virginia 253
   Desperately Seeking What's His Nickname.........................255
   Why I Don't Like Going to Meetings.....................................257
   Taking Your Shot Best...259
   A January Night Scene 261
   Whistle While You. . .Whatever 263
   Never Give a Sucker—Period 265
   Report Card Day..267
   Memories of Finger Painting 269
   A Critique of Perfectly Good Reason.................................... 271
   The Art of Analogy...273
   Storms of All Kinds...275

WATCHING PEOPLE

A Trip to the Zoo

I took my family a few years ago to a big zoo in a suburb of Chicago. Let me tell you.

The most interesting species we saw was *Gigantis vulgaris*. This species, which does not exist in the wild much any more, wears baseball caps, tee shirts with lewd mottoes, and either shorts or jeans.

The young of this species fall into two groups. The adolescents wear old rags and huge sneakers, and must eat constantly. They look tired, and some even appeared to be stuck together. The pre-adolescents, usually named either Jason or Brittany, may be identified by their tendency to scream whenever placed near my ear. Either ear.

The adult *G. vulgaris* instruct the young in the way they should go. One tall, red-haired adult male hauled his young up to an exhibit and trumpeted: "**NOW JASON, THIS HERE IS THE *COYOTE*! THEY USED TO BE *MILLIONS* OF THESE ALL OVER THE AMERICAN WEST, BUT NOW THEY'RE NEARLY *EXTINCT*! THIS HERE MIGHT BE THE *LAST* COYOTE YOU WILL EVER SEE!**"

He said this while stationed directly in front of a big sign that said this here is actually an African jackal.

I believe, too, that he mispronounced "coyote." He pronounced it KYE-OAT. I used to live in Oklahoma, and there I learned to pronounce it DAMKYE-YODY. And, by the way, coyotes are endangered only in the ambitions of farmers and ranchers.

But it's OK: Jason wasn't paying attention anyway. He was pretending to shoot the jackal, aiming down his arm and saying "Pcheu! Pcheu!" The jackal was lounging under a tree, nearly asleep, probably having been shot this way many times before.

This unconcerned attitude was pretty common. The gorilla, for instance, appeared to have just got home from work, and was watching the imaginary news on an imaginary TV, lolling in the crotch of a tree with his arms spread out. He appeared to have something on his mind, but we couldn't tell what. Whatever it was, he was obviously certain he was right about it.

We could tell exactly what the tiger was thinking, however: he was figuring how to get out of his cage and eat some of us. And there was a pregnant rhinoceros, but we didn't try to figure out what she was thinking because she had been pregnant already nearly two years, and was clearly in *no mood*. We kind of looked down and walked on past as quietly as we could.

Some of the animals appeared–well, not really smart. None of the ostriches, for instance, had figured out how to groom its hair, so they all looked kind of dopey. They appeared to have just got up, and were still trying to figure out whether it was Saturday. (It was.)

There were several species of little rat-like fellows that bustled around all day working at top speed on something or other. If they had thought about it at all, they would have seen that there was nothing much they really *needed* to be doing. A quiet talk with the gorilla might have calmed them down.

We all had a good time (except for the pregnant rhinoceros). The polar bears were cool, even in the heat. The giraffe was supercilious, the lion emphatic, the crocodiles hideous. The monkeys injected a streak of fun and the jaguars a touch of royalty. The bears made fun of the spectators, and the spectators made fun of the orangutan. The porcupine tended to its business. People spent money, and the gnu snorted at them for it. Everyone, including *G. vulgaris*, did what came naturally to random species thrown together on an idle afternoon.

The zoo is fun. You just have to keep figuring out who's on exhibit.

Finding Faces

Recently I was in a certain kind of room, engaged in a certain exercise that required me to stand still for a few minutes facing the wall. Well, you know. As I stood there, feeling better all the time, I noticed a figure among the little bumps and swirls on the wall. It seemed to have just a little curve, kind of like a hairline, with another curve underneath like eyebrows. There were some spots, another little line or two, and from these the impression of a face emerged.

This face seemed to be interested in something, looking down and to my left, and maybe talking. You've seen the expression often on people's faces when they are fully engaged in a conversation. It was a lively, interested and interesting little piece of human face.

But then I looked away, and when I tried to find it again, I couldn't. All I could see was random lines and spots. I determined to examine those to see whether there were other faces, and sure enough, I found another one. This was only a few lines, to be sure: a nose, I think, part of a jawline, and some lips. It would have been part of the face of a tall person, like a high school friend of my son's, looking this time to my right, appearing to listen to a distant sound. Nice kid, as I recall. His attitude appeared to imply the existence of someone else in another part of a little world of marks on a wall where he existed, and I don't.

Now, my time there was limited: it would have been unseemly, even suspicious, for me to stand there longer than I needed to, so I felt constrained to leave.

But I thought about it. I began to try to find these faces around me: in the pile of the carpet, in the leaves and branches of trees around my house, in the pebbles in my driveway, in my New Year's black-eyed peas. Well, not really there, but you know what I mean.

And I have discovered the most wonderful thing: the world is full of faces. Fascinating faces. Faces we would like to talk with, to know something about. Faces that reflect human attitudes of all kinds—smiling, sneering, sometimes afraid, sometimes delighted, sometimes telling a joke, sometimes worrying with a friend about a problem. Faces like those of people we know. And these faces appear to be reacting to other people whom we can't see. The world is full not only of faces, but of other worlds.

When you get used to finding these faces, you realize you don't need much of the face to recognize it. You don't need all the familiar minimal lines of eyebrows, eyes, nose, lips. Sometimes just a certain curve of a twig will intersect with another twig like a mouth and an eyebrow relating to one another in a chuckling squint. Sometimes all it takes is a spot for an eye turned just right in relation to a smudge of an eyebrow to express the sudden burst of love a mother feels toward her baby.

Now, I'm not nuts. I know perfectly well that these are just lines, twigs, leaves, pebbles. They don't give me instructions to commit crimes, nor do they intimate that the world is about to burn up.

What they do instead is remind me that the human personality is infinitely complicated, infinitely full of variety, infinitely interested in itself. These little moments of discovery and recognition are revelations of the faces of humankind sharing its feelings, and rejoicing in its ability to share its feelings. Loving the world and life, and sharing that love. Exploring, investigating, puzzling, and sharing those feelings. Talking among ourselves.

We fill the earth; we fill each other. We are boundlessly capable of adapting to every ounce of the world, and of interpenetrating each other's minds and awareness. If we just take the trouble to look, we can find ourselves everywhere. We love being together because we see ourselves in others, and we love being alone because we can find ourselves and others all around us in the world.

It's a good company to keep. Take a look at some uninteresting corner of the world. See who is at home. See what I mean.

See what I mean?

Fun At The Movies

"Anyway, I told her, 'Don't get it took off. If God didn't want you to have a bump on your nose, He wouldn't have put it there,' but she said she wanted to because when she gets tired she accidentally steers by it, and it makes her veer left. Said she walked into a Chevy Blazer last week and bruised her knee."

This, or a conversation like it, is usually going on before the movie begins. It's hard not to eavesdrop. Meanwhile, a pair of mature ladies ventures down the aisle.

"Where would you like to sit? Here? Down here?"

"Well, I don't really mind. Where would you like to sit? Does this look good to you?"

"Let's just sit back here, I guess. Right down here is fine, if that's all right with you."

With only ten people in the entire theater, there are plenty of seats. I want to holler: "Why don't you each take four or five just to be sure?" But that would be unmannerly, of course, so I sit still.

Also I am hoping my polite wife will continue preparing meals.

A group of teenagers enters, giggling about something, hands over mouths. Each carries a lifetime supply of pop in a plastic cup and a tub of popcorn. They sit dangerously near the screen. What must the movie look like from down there?

But then I remember: they provide their own entertainment. The movie is just a diverting backdrop. OK by me. Fortunately I'm a little deaf, so as far as I know, they are silent.

Good thing I'm deaf, too, because when the movie comes on, the volume of sound lifts me out of my seat. It comes from all sides!

Paul Cox

What used to be a peaceful fold in a curtain has erupted into violent crashing and zinging! The world may be ending!

No, that's not it. It's an ad for a restaurant, or a truck dealership, or an investment plan.

My wife and I don't like ads at the beginning of movies, but I do enjoy the previews.

It's like watching four or five mini-movies. You almost figure out what the story is about. Stars do interesting things. You see and hear explosions. The only difference from the feature movie is that the previews are shorter. What fun!

Then a solemn moment: the announcement that we are not to litter or smoke in the auditorium. We all take note. The teenagers stop giggling and give rapt attention: you can see that they are vowing internally not to litter! Not to smoke!

Meanwhile the conversationalists rumble on. Gardening plans, church gossip, child-rearing crises are all brought up and resolved. The momentum of the conversation seems strong: I am afraid I may miss some of the subtle opening dialogue.

And suddenly the movie begins. The sound track, formerly deafening, becomes even louder. The sound is so powerful that we experience it as a solid.

People are dancing, drinking champagne. They're under a tent in a garden, laughing, dressed formally.

Must be a wedding. Here's a white-haired man smiling at a six-year old girl in a pretty dress. A grandmother in black looking indulgent. A caterer fretting. A mischievous child swiping sips of champagne.

Who's that with curly hair? Must be the bride—movie brides always have curly hair, I think. Or else the Other Woman, also always curly-haired.

The groom seems to have extra bones in his face. Looks intensely at the curly-haired woman. Hm.

Ah, yes. Must be a love story. I settle back, and soon my wife wakes me. It's time for dinner.

A good afternoon.

A Consumer's Complaint

Years ago I patronized a good men's clothing store. I did so reluctantly, because I don't like buying clothes, but when I needed a suit, I went there. The people were pleasant, the clothes were fine, the prices were reasonable.

Most of all, I could find what I wanted pretty easily. Usually that was a gray suit, and if not, then a blue suit. I am a dull kind of guy.

But one day, needing a suit, I walked into this store and my blood froze: I saw ladies wear. Silky blouses, as I recall, and a few scarves. The manager assured me it was just a few things. The parent company wanted to see what would happen.

I knew perfectly well what would happen, and that is why my blood froze. Within six months I was completely unable to buy anything at the store. All the men's suits were squeezed back into one little corner, and there were very few of them. The prices went up. I had to quit shopping there.

I'm sure they didn't care. They probably made more money selling ladies wear, and I can't really fault them for that. Ladies buy more clothes, I guess.

But it is part of a phenomenon I've noticed: whenever there is a good product, or a good store, it changes. It gets cuter or more complicated, and then it just disappears. What was good to buy becomes no longer good to sell, for some reason.

A few years ago I started using some kind of goop to comb my hair with. It worked pretty well and I bought it regularly. I did this for a couple of years, and suddenly it was gone. Couldn't buy it anywhere.

Paul Cox

What I think happens is that the manufacturers see they have a good thing. So they figure to make it better. They introduce exciting new flavors, new sizes, new formulas. They push these, figuring to build on the success of the original product to conquer new worlds.

But in their zeal they stop thinking about the original good product.

And why not? That is a problem they have finished solving. Conquering this market is no longer interesting. The fun is in seeing what *else* you can do with the product.

So they fiddle with what was perfectly good until they get it scrambled up. Then they conclude: this product is a failure, or this store has to be reinvented. We have to try something else entirely different.

Recently I needed some dental floss. I went into a new, large pharmacy, figuring this would be easy. It is a modern, up-to-date store. A clean, well-lighted place, if you will forgive the snide allusion.

I found the dental floss section, which was about six or eight feet of display, and began to look. To my shock and dismay, there was no plain, ordinary, unflavored, unwaxed dental floss to be had. Not one inch of it.

I could have got waxed grape flavored dental floss, or mint dental tape, or something in a cool stretchy fabric. But why? Why would I want grape flavored dental floss? Do I not know the difference between flossing my teeth and eating dessert?

Simple dental floss was nowhere in the store. Not believing it could be true, I asked and got the smiling shrug. I went across the street to the grocery store, and there quickly purchased exactly what I wanted.

But this just gives me another concern, actually. If the grocery store carries my kind of dental floss, what will happen if I go there to buy potatoes? I worry.

A Southerner Remembers Heat

There's a special relationship between southern people and hot weather. Something about the blood, maybe, or the organization of the nervous system.

When I was young, growing up in eastern North Carolina and tidewater Virginia, summer was a pleasant exercise in managing our response to the heat. There was no air-conditioning, of course, so handling hot weather was serious business.

One strategy favored by ladies was to hold a glass of cool lemonade or iced tea against the inside of one's wrist. The idea was that the blood passes very near the surface of the skin at that point, so you could sort of refrigerate your blood that way.

Now, it didn't work, of course. Not really: all that really happened was that the lemonade or iced tea got warm faster.

But that didn't matter. What did matter was that it was an attempt, and that the work of a resourceful lady was to hold her glass against her wrist and discuss the blood-cooling theory with similarly-inclined friends.

A strategy that did work was to open the house at night, trapping cool night air, and shut it up during the day. As I kid I thought closed windows in hot weather were clearly contra-indicated—I mean, a bad idea—but I was wrong. Cunning housewives understood and discussed this trick, and it worked, at least for most of the morning.

Note what these two devices had in common. One didn't work and the other did, but they were both perfectly valid because they provided matter for polite conversation. It wasn't so much that people talked about the weather itself. It was a given that every day in summer would be hot and humid. No, the conversation was about managing one's response to the weather. The difference is subtle, but important.

Because in the long run, that's what beat the heat—sitting calmly with friends making quiet, collected conversation. Dealing with the heat as one dealt with a misbehaving cousin in a far-off city or a little turmoil of church politics. You talked about such things in settling ways, and kept them from disturbing your serenity.

I've lived in the north, where it also gets very hot in summer, even though the hot season is shorter. Northern people, who have to deal with very severe winters, think summer is just another season.

Their response to summer heat is to try to beat it, to resist it, to complain about it as if something is wrong. They know that it will ultimately be balanced by a cold as bitter as the heat is oppressive. So they jitter back and forth among the seasons, never really belonging to any one.

A southerner, though, knows that hot weather is what life is really all about. Southerners know how to relax in warm weather, to let it settle in among our bones and clear away any residual frosts that might ever have been there.

At least, we used to.

Air-conditioning has changed the way we relate to hot weather. Now we can just shut the heat outside. We can go from a cool house to a cool car to a cool office without ever feeling the sun. Southern cities now have passageways linking buildings that allow shoppers to go from store to store and office workers to go from office to office without ever having to go outside.

And I suppose that's good. There's no sense wasting energy pining over the past. Air conditioning is, I suppose, more healthful.

But you know, it isn't the heat I miss. It's the gentle discipline of contriving calm.

Buying Clothes

I don't enjoy shopping for clothes. The problem, as I now see it, is that I already *have* clothes. When I go to a store to buy some pants, I will be wearing pants, and I will have other pants at home that I could have worn if I had chosen to. Almost at any time when I buy clothes, I could have bought them a week earlier, or a week later, and it wouldn't have mattered. Buying clothes just never seems to me something particularly urgent.

My wife is better than I at investing clothes purchases with a level of urgency. First, she never "wants" clothes: she "needs" them. Second, she doesn't think of an article of clothing as a hat or a shirt (which she thinks is called a "blouse," but that's another topic). No, she thinks of any given article of clothing as an element in an ensemble—a little piece of decorative art of which all the elements must be strictly coordinated for color, style, weight, design, and usually price.

Any element can work, like a tablespoon of sourdough culture, as the starter. Let us say that at some time I foolishly give her a handkerchief. Something with strawberries.

Now, she does not have anything else featuring strawberries. So she will say to me: "I need a skirt to match that lovely strawberry handkerchief you gave me."

I will say in vain: "Oh, you don't need to bother with that—it was only a harmless and poorly conceived literary allusion." But it doesn't matter what I might say, because her having told me she "needs" such a skirt has constituted negotiation, agreement, and a grant of unlimited purchasing authority.

Soon she has a box with the name of a store on it in swoopy script. It contains a skirt with a strawberry figure. "See! I found just the skirt! Isn't it exciting!" It costs $165. This expense, however, is not something that could have been avoided, like retirement. No, the skirt was a necessity, given the existence of the handkerchief. Which, by the way, retailed for $1.27.

This story may labor on without us from here: the skirt requires a "blouse," which has to have a scarf, and that mandates shoes, obviously, and these cannot be used with an improper purse. And clearly such an elegant ensemble is only correct *on the surface* until there is matching underwear.

So an important principle of clothes buying is the urgency of building ensembles. No blouse is an island.

Another form of urgency is seasonal. Here's what I mean. When I go out and find the weather getting chilly, I may think: I need a new scarf. I mention this to my wife, who says: "You can't buy a scarf now. They were in season six months ago."

"But six months ago was spring."

"Exactly. That's when they put these things out. If you don't have your winter wardrobe by June, you can forget it."

I usually go to the store anyway and locate a perfectly serviceable scarf. But that is because I miss the point, which is: women obey a seasonal imperative. They can't wait around about buying clothes, because time and tide wait for no man, as King Knut's wife reminded him so long ago.

And there is another imperative: sales. My wife, a diligent economist, mourns any sale that she is unable to honor with a purchase. She believes that if she buys heavily when merchandise is on sale, she will be training merchants to offer low prices. We argue about this.

"You should buy things when they are on sale!" she suggests. "That's the way to save money!"

"I should not let merchants decide when I need to buy things, and what things I should buy," I respond. "That's the way to go broke."

I think some of my dislike for buying clothes springs from my childhood. My mother would take me to the store and tell Mrs. Yancy, a woman of roughly her generation, what I needed. Mrs. Yancy would begin with measurement: a tape around my waist first, involving a quick little embrace which was over before I was alert enough to avoid it.

Then suddenly, measuring tape in hand. Mrs. Yancy kneels and pokes me with her thumb. She extends the tape to my cuff with the other hand, measuring what she delicately calls "the crouch." Of course, surrounded by mannequins in underwear, and caught off guard by this strange woman, my body reacts with a lurching spasm that involves bending at the waist and lifting a knee. Inside my clothes I flinch extravagantly. Mrs. Yancy, who has probably seen this before—although at the time I supposed myself unique in my physical sensitivities—goes on measuring my crouch, and tells my mother she has a "nice pant" that might fit with just a little alteration.

This experience serves to close down my active participation in this entire process. I am along now only as an example of what size I am. My mother selects, decides, evaluates, pays. I carry. She does, of course, nominally involve me: "Isn't this a nice little blouse, Paul?"

I only nod and hurry back to whatever daydream is protecting my integrity at the moment.

I have tried, as an adult, having my wife present as I buy clothes. But it does not work well. She is, of course, better at it than I am. She has more practice, she enjoys it, and she believes it is an all right thing to do. I, on the other hand, must shun the offers of my unconscious to supply me with diverting daydreams. And I don't have much practice—either at buying clothes or avoiding daydreaming.

But when she is along, I feel uncomfortable. No, that's not exactly it: I feel comfortable. I find myself agreeing to extravagant purchases, like socks and underwear, that I would normally never indulge in. I find myself considering two pairs of pants, and matching neckties. Blazers. I find myself using words like "need" and "ought." I find myself enjoying buying clothes.

And that's just wrong.

Spies. Sunlight. Diabetes. Guacamole.

I knew a guy a while back who claimed to be a retired spy. Or agent, or intelligence operative or whatever. He was pointedly vague about terminology—as if the phrase "pointedly vague" could mean anything.

He told us about the last time he was in Moscow. Said he spent a whole Sunday afternoon lying on the side of a hill overlooking the city with a fellow operative and some binoculars.

"Doing what?" I asked.

"Better not say."

I didn't take it any further, but I wondered why he had brought it up in the first place.

This conversation happened in a Mexican restaurant one Saturday evening. My industrious wife and I had spent all afternoon planting some shrubbery around our house, and were, if you'll pardon the pun, totally bushed.

It had been a record hot day in Indiana, where we lived: the sun bright, brutally hot, and unrelenting. Over a hundred degrees, as I recall. The soil around our house was dense, hard, sticky clay full of rocks.

But we had worked all afternoon, and by evening were witless from it all: the sun seemed to have occupied our heads, and was burning everything in there. We had just time to shower before our friends picked us up to go to this Mexican restaurant for dinner.

But we made it, and here we were talking about spying. My friend Percy (not his real name, of course; I have to be careful) went so far as to NAME NAMES. I capitalize this to conform with current conventions of usage. When a person NAMES NAMES, it is shocking, see.

He named Frank, JoAnne, and somebody named Wally, although he said those weren't their real names. He spoke mysteriously of a Mr. Simpson, who made some devices.

"Devices? What do the devices do?"

"Better not say," he explained. "Simpson was from MIT."

About this time Percy's wife, a diabetic, began to get kind of spacey. Percy (not his real name) snapped his fingers.

"Waiter. Señor. Orange juice, please. Right away," my friend ordered.

"Si." The waiter hurried off, eyebrows working.

"I OK," his wife mumbled. "Don't nee juice. Stuff."

"Drink it!" he ordered. "You need it."

"'M OK. 'M OK. Leemy lone."

I sensed a crisis brewing. What does a trained spy—or operative—do in a case of a diabetic problem in a Mexican restaurant? Is there a special set of secret moves?

"Judy! Drink the juice!"

That must be the technique, because Judy muttered something grumbly, made a face, drank the orange juice, and stuck out her tongue at her husband.

Pretty soon she perked up a little, and the crisis passed. I wondered whether her name was really Judy.

The guy, meanwhile, was saying something about secret codes, or maybe about submarines or some special kind of ink.

About then the waiter came back with some excellent guacamole—chunky pieces of avocado, not too creamy, fresh onion, a little lime juice—and a basket of warm chips with a heavy red salsa.

Off in the distance a large man in an ornamented black sombrero began playing a guitar quietly, and people at a nearby table laughed pleasantly. I felt just fine.

And suddenly I lost all interest in spies, false names, orange juice, and codes. The sun was finally beginning mercifully to set in my head and we had some good food.

"Lawn's going to look good," my wife said quietly. Yep, I thought so too, and I felt just fine.

I was finding reality rather more interesting than spies at the moment. Whatever their names might be.

My Wall Companion

Having had one, I recommend that everybody find a good wall companion.

Here's what I mean.

A few years ago I began to develop some hearing difficulties. No big deal, but I noticed that in crowded places I couldn't understand what people were saying.

I'm told that this is common, actually. And it has never become much worse. My obliging wife always orders when we go to a restaurant because most of the time I have little or no idea what it is the server (or waitperson or dinner consultant or whatever the term is now) might be saying.

Once I nearly got thrown out of a high class restaurant in Mexico for yelling WHAT?! at a waiter. My tone of voice was somewhat out of character for the place; heavy moustaches twitched indignantly.

So anyway, I developed this little sensory shortfall that was a nuisance in some social situations. One-on-one, I'm fine. Thirty-on-one, I'm bewildered.

I was a member at the time of a small church that always ended our services with a coffee hour. The people were quite nice—very much like a family—and we enjoyed each other immensely.

But the coffee hours put a double-whammy on me. Coffee gives me the heebie-jeebies, and I couldn't make sense out of the conversation. What was pleasant and valuable fellowship for everyone else was less than fun for me.

Somehow, though, I managed to strike a deal with a friend, Gene. We were good friends, and saw eye to eye on many subjects.

More important for this account, he apparently had the same problem as I did (although we never discussed it), so somehow we wound up each Sunday standing against a wall together.

Neither of us said anything after "Morning, how you doing." We just stood at our wall. For as long as it took.

You see, if you stand against a wall alone, people assume that you're lonely and need companionship. They will approach you and say something or other, probably something nice.

Maybe they're trying to get you to drink coffee. I don't know, because I generally can't make it out.

You want to be polite, but it's hard. If you shout WHAT?! at them, they may react as the maitre d' at the Mexican restaurant did, and try to retaliate in some way.

So a stratagem is valuable to immunize you against the friendly-intentioned person who tries to include you in the fun.

That's what a wall companion provides. Other people saw Gene and me standing against a wall, smiling comfortably, and not looking as if we needed help.

They assumed, I think, that we were engaged in weighty conversation. Or maybe they didn't assume anything, but just noticed that we were paired up satisfactorily, and left us alone.

All in all, then, Gene and I spent many silent hours simply standing together against a wall. On some level, I think we communicated during that time: something about patience, the importance of quiet in one's life, something deep and richly significant in a mysterious turtle-wisdom mode.

Mostly, though, we just stood there. It wasn't an exercise in a meditative discipline; it was a clever way to avoid the fun without spurning it.

Once the coffee hour was over, we helped pick up the cups, and probably even took our proper turn washing them from time to time. We went away refreshed and pleased by the morning's fellowship, just as much as those who had sipped coffee and talked.

A good wall companion is hard to find, but I can tell you, he's worth the effort.

Family Portraits

We were visiting friends recently, when I heard my wife cackle. "It's us!" she laughed.

She was in the hall looking at a picture. It was a family portrait of our host and hostess with their two sons, taken about 25 years ago by Olan Mills. In the photo the young parents are dressed in the styles of the time, including large polyester lapels and wide ties. Their sons, now married adults, were boys, with carefree (but carefully posed) grins.

"You could just paste our faces in and it would be the same picture we have," my wife said, and she was right. We have the same family portrait, with the same poses, same clothes, same grave looking parents (us as we were then), same carefree (but carefully posed) kids.

And I'm willing to bet we're not the only ones. Here's my advice: keep those photos safe. Make copies for all your kids.

There are other family portraits on our wall. One of our favorites shows my father's family as they appeared in about 1915 or so. They sit carefully arranged by size outside their home, a plain frame farmhouse on which some of the siding boards are horizontal and others vertical.

There are 11 kids. The younger boys wear dark knee-length trousers, stylish white shirts, and wide, floppy bow ties; and the older boys, tall and strong, wear dark suits with neat gray four-in-hand ties knotted perfectly. The younger girls are dressed in a slightly feminized version of what their young brothers have on;

and the older girls, looking serious and worthy, wear handsome dark dresses.

My grandfather, whom I never knew, is wearing a snappy plaid suit and a big moustache, and my grandmother a stately full dress, fitting for the matriarch of such a clan.

My family never gets together without reviewing this photograph, lingering over the odd names (all the children's names began with the letter Z for some reason), pointing out interesting details. My father, for instance, was caught at the moment of scratching his left calf with his right big toenail.

I've seen similar photographs of other families from about the same time: same clothing, same poses. There are probably hundreds or thousands of these family portraits arranged, posed, and snapped by travelling photographers with trunks full of "suitable" clothing in all sizes.

My mother's small family had one, too. I expect small-town and rural families all over the south, maybe all over the country, have photographs just like these.

We look into the faces and eyes of those children so long ago, whom we last saw as elderly grandparents at their funerals, and we wonder: what did they see? Who did they think they were? What colors, sights, ideas were in their heads? What news did they hear and respond to? What made them laugh? What were they doing just before the picture was taken? What did they do just after?

We look at their parents, younger in 1915 than we are now, and try to imagine what they worried about, how they solved their problems, what they hoped for.

It's hard to realize that some day our children's children will look at and muse over these Olan Mills family portraits of us. Hard to imagine that we will be the figures of legend and wonder for them that our grandparents are for us.

Decades from now they will wonder what problems worried us. If we could tell them, they would probably wonder why we ever thought those were problems.

Silly old family portraits. Innocent, old-fashioned, optimistic, stiffly posed, a little embarrassing. (Did I really look that pompous back then?)

Do you suppose the photographers were aware that they were creating a national treasure at least as great as Mount Rushmore?

Becoming Bda

I have a little problem, but I think I may have found the solution. I'd like to discuss it with you, however, before I go ahead.

Our only granddaughter is now about six months old. For about a year, people, including my helpful wife, have been pestering me: what do I want this grandchild to call me? Granddaddy? Gramps? Pop-pop? Grandpa?

There were several other possibilities, all with their plusses and their minuses. As for me, though, I preferred to leave it to the grandchild: whatever she wanted to call me would be OK with me.

That was an unpopular view. No, I should designate a title, so she could learn it early on.

But I was reluctant. What if I chose, say, "Venerable Grandsire," and she thought of me instead as "Grampa"? Wouldn't that have implications for personality development (not just hers)?

When she was about two or three months old, we visited her in Pittsburgh, and an unusual thing happened.

Rebecca—the granddaughter—was lolling around as kids that age do, and began speaking. She said: "Grdddddddddoooo HUYYK!" Said it over and over.

Now, I understand a little Baby, so I knew what she meant. "Grdddddddddoooo" means "This is a fun thing to say," and "HUYYK" means "I'm having a good time."

(A quick pronunciation guide. "Grdddddddddoooo" is pronounced on a quickly descending scale. "HUYYK" is pronounced on the intake of air, not the output.)

Shortly after, while visiting in my lap, Becky looked at me solemnly, touched my nose and distinctly said: "BDA! HUYKK!"

Now, we know what HUYYK means from before. And I'm pretty confident that "BDA" is the name with which she was christening me. I am BDA, so far as she is concerned, and that's OK with me.

This weekend Becky is bringing her parents here for my ever-youthful wife's birthday observance, and this matter of how she should address me continues to come up, as if unsettled. But I had an inspiration. I conceived a cunning strategem.

I work in an ABC store, see. For non-North Carolinians, that's a state-controlled liquor store. I stock the shelves. It's a good job: a clean, well run store. Pleasant people to work with and pleasant customers. I enjoy it.

As I worked the other day I realized I was surrounded by excellent grandparent names. I began to think of appropriate choices.

"Old Grand-Dad" might be a little too obvious. "Lord Calvert"? "Grey Goose"? "Ancient Age"? How about "Kahlua"?

Maybe not "Smirnoff." Certainly not "Old Crow."

Other names came to mind. Think, for instance, of the fun Becky could have in kindergarten telling her classmates she had gone to North Carolina for a traditional Thanksgiving dinner with her Grandmommy and Jose Cuervo.

Right to the head of the class. You know it.

So I discussed it with my wife. She's the one, after all, who has been after me to designate a title for myself. Her reaction was immediate and emphatic: "That's a terrible thing to do to your granddaughter, teaching her the names of liquor! Absolutely not!"

My strategy was going to work! "Oh," I said with a forlorn air. "I guess then, if it can't be one of those, we'll just have to go with . . .."

And there was no longer any discussion. I think Bda is going to work just fine. My wife even conceived a feminine form for herself. We are Mna and Bda. Settled.

HUYYK!

Who's In Charge Here?

Not too many years ago we all knew who was in charge. It was Howard Cosell. If you didn't believe it, you could just ask him.

Howard Cosell got to decide things like what the correct nicknames for various athletes should be. Remember "the Juice"? You don't hear that much anymore. Remember how he assigned Sugar Ray Robinson's nickname to Ray Leonard? (Mistake, I thought.)

It was great when Cosell was around, because he could tell us what to think and explain the rules for us. I remember his shouting at least fifty times during one boxing match, "You must pronate the glove!" Who else could have said that? Who else would bother to? And why so many times?

Before Cosell, Eisenhower pretty much had things under control, and at one point, when Cosell was fading, Alexander Haig claimed to be in charge, but he flamed out on us. Other candidates to succeed Cosell have included Donald Trump, Jerry Falwell, Jane Fonda and Speaker Newt. But none of them ever quite took.

Michael Jordan could have taken over, but he's too genteel. Jesse Ventura wants to, but he isn't genteel enough. Barbara Walters is genteel, but then she tilts her head and says something sappy. Oprah has the talent, but she is too preoccupied with weightier matters (sorry).

So the world bumps along, leaderless, adrift.

PEOPLEWATCHING

I have often been tempted to take charge. I don't know whether I could do as good a job as Howard Cosell, but here are some things I would tend to immediately.

First, I would explain once and for all that sno-cones are a waste of money.

Then I would clear up the confusion about Elvis Presley: he's dead.

I would explain how we don't really need special stores to sell Christmas decorations all year around.

I would assign clever nicknames not to sports figures, but to business leaders. Ted Turner could be called, let's say, "Turpentine." Why not? Bill Gates would be "Mikey" (that's short for Microsoft, see). I would not give Donald Trump a nickname unless he called me and asked nicely. Fat chance.

I would let everyone know how North Carolina barbecue is under-rated relative to Memphis or Texas barbecues, and I would make public fun of anyone who put beans in chili. I would encourage the use of garlic in nearly everything (except perhaps lemonade).

I would decree that nobody had to wear neckties ever again, and would encourage women to trade in their high heels for whatever else they might prefer. I don't know about panty hose: I might not say anything there, as I am unqualified.

I would direct that all towns and cities must have downtown hardware stores, soda fountains, and barbershops. I would shame movie theaters into turning down the volume.

You can guess what I would do about gangsta rap, I expect. Harrumph.

I would encourage screen porches. I would direct that half the population should take a walk after dinner through their neighborhoods, and the other half should sit on their screen porches and chat with the walkers as they pass.

If I were in charge, nobody would throw trash around. Nobody would take more than 10 items into the express checkout lane. Nobody would talk during a movie. Nobody would throw the extra high note ("o'er the la-and of the free-EEEE!") into the national anthem. Nobody would play car radios loud enough to be heard in other cars. Nobody would be impatient with old people or harsh with young people.

And if you supinate the glove, I won't say anything.

What Do You Say to That, Sir?

If you asked my father a question, you usually got an answer.

Of course, my father didn't know all the answers. He felt, however, that he was supposed to answer if anyone asked him something.

I don't recall ever hearing him say, "I don't know."

Now, my father wasn't a liar. He was an honorable, decent man who grew up in an age when adult males were expected to have answers.

So when he invented an answer, he wasn't lying. He was just fulfilling, as well as he could, an obligation. Best if the response was at least reasonable, but the critical thing was to respond one way or another.

Naturally, we kids could always tell when he didn't know.

We thought our mother didn't realize what was happening. "Thad," she would say, "Why does. . .?"

He would immediately say, "Well, because, you see. . . ." and invent a transparent answer. We kids sighed and rolled our eyes sagely, but our mother gazed as if fascinated and enlightened.

At the time I thought she was infinitely gullible. Now, from a more mature perspective, I see that she was actually just loyal and loving.

Recently a friend and I were talking about calling technical support phone numbers with computer questions. She said she could tell instantly when the "support technician" actually knew even less than she does.

It's frustrating, she said, to hold on the line an hour for someone, and then to realize immediately that the person you've waited for has no clue, but gives you anyhow the solution to some other problem that's easier.

I thought immediately of my father, and wondered: what's this compulsion to answer, even when you don't know what you're talking about?

My father felt it because that's how he was brought up. The support technician is hired to feel it—because the company he or she works for subscribes to my father's view. Any old answer will do, as long as you say something.

But then she said something else really fascinating. She had learned to tell whether a person is over thirty: if you know right away whether he or she has good answers, then that person is under thirty. Something in the voice.

I think that's a pretty astute observation, and it brings up a fascinating thought.

Maybe what happens is that somewhere in the process of maturation we develop the reflex for using language strategically. We speak not to express our thoughts and feelings, but to achieve a result.

And perhaps it's that strategic use of language that compels people answer questions they don't understand. We want to maintain a position of authority, and the way to do that is always to have an answer handy.

We are all used to strategic language. It's what we dislike about politicians. It's why we discount advertising claims.

We like to quote part of a phrase, "Out of the mouths of babes. ..." The phrase implies that unmonitored childlike babble is wiser, truer, more honest than careful adult language. That it's more moral than adult caginess.

I disagree, however. Speaking strategically is not really bad. We all do it, and most people are reasonably decent. It's naïve to hope others won't do what we all do.

There's no sense expecting the world to be different from what it is. People are going to speak strategically; they're going to pretend to know, sometimes, when they don't.

I like my mother's approach: if my husband's a good person, then I'll go with it a little. She lived to be 91.

Fleshy Things on the Beach

Something is not quite right about elephant seals. These are those big fleshy things with bulbous noses that lie on the sand in California. No, you're thinking of people. These are something different.

Recently my curious wife and I visited California and happened on a beachful of both: elephant seals and tourists watching elephant seals.

Elephant seals (you can't imagine how tired I am of typing this phrase) look like huge slugs that have died on the beach. Hundreds of them; it's a melancholy sight. Then they move, but only a little, and not often.

Sometimes they flop over to a neighbor, if they see they can inconvenience the neighbor that way. Actually, they don't so much flop *to* a neighbor as *onto* the neighbor. Without asking.

Sometimes they serenade with a kind of illiterate rasping HONK that means, in seal, "Tra la, what a beautiful afternoon!"

Sometimes they flip sand onto their own backs and into their neighbors' eyes.

Sometimes they look at the tourists in frank surprise.

The tourists, for their part, are in awe of the elephant seals. How can such big things be so lazy? How can such lazy things be so ugly? How can such ugly things be so interesting? This is what the tourists are thinking.

Also the elephant seals.

There is a sign at the beach that says: Don't feed the elephant seals. Don't get close to them. Don't touch them. Don't offer them money for tricks. Don't name your dog after them. Don't argue theology with them. Don't bug them in any way.

Well, I didn't write it down, but it was a lot of rules like that.

The elephant seals generally obey these rules, but not all the tourists do. Some try to feed the elephant seals bagels. Of course, to the elephant seals, it looks as if the tourist is offering them an arm for a snack.

Fortunately, however, the elephant seals are too lazy to eat.

Really good bagels are hard to get in California, anyway.

Occasionally an elephant seal decides to go somewhere. Only problem is, of course, that they really can't. They don't have legs, and their arms are just little silly flippers.

So they make up for it by acting like a kid who has got wound up in the covers: they just start flopping the direction they want to go. This is not easy for them, and pretty soon they forget just why they wanted to go there anyway.

And it really doesn't matter, because there isn't much of anywhere for them to go anyway.

At this point they start a lovely song, like the one quoted above. The tourists applaud, but the other elephant seals have higher musical standards. They just lie there.

The more ambitious ones stare at the performer; the rest are annoyed, and don't open their eyes. Maybe they flip sand on themselves and their neighbors.

Near the elephant seal beach is the famous Hearst Castle, where the concept of bad taste originated.

And, I regret to say, flourished.

This establishment, according to the docent, started out as a little camping lodge, and wound up as a gigantic set of buildings with swimming pools, movie stars, palm trees, flowers, zebras and ostriches, imported trees, and statues of naked persons.

Yours six times daily for only $4.

The same tourists who plagued the elephant seals went to the Hearst Castle.

The elephant seals had better things to do, and, one supposes, did them.

As I said, California is a strange and wonderful place.

Oh, did I forget to say that?

HONK. Flop.

Why I Do Not Want Contact Lenses

The trouble with contact lenses is that they deprive you of an important expressive resource.

Here's what I mean. Imagine a situation in which you must make certain that someone understands you perfectly, and realizes the importance of what you are saying.

To achieve this certainty, you should whip off your glasses and brandish them so that one earpiece points toward the other person. Now stare at the person as you talk, bobbing the glasses up and down once for every word you say.

This! will! drive! your! point! home!. The other person not only hears what you're saying, but is compelled to recognize its importance. When other rhetorical strategies fail, good glasses management gets spectacular results. (Forgive me.)

Or suppose somebody is explaining something interesting to you. You want to signal your fascination, but you don't want to interrupt.

Simply take off your glasses. Hold them just below your chin, tilt your head a little, and screw up your eyebrows. Try it. See there: you have just said, "Well, I'll be darned" without uttering a syllable.

Sometimes you need a good, sturdy pair of glasses.

Suppose you are sitting across the table from someone disagreeing about something. The other person says something that you want to characterize as outrageously false. You want to be emphatic about this: there are points to be scored.

So what do you do? You whip off your glasses and toss them onto the table. If you are skillful and practiced, you will toss them with a little flip of the wrist that makes the glasses rotate just a bit when they hit the table.

See there? You don't even have to say anything. In all the world's known languages, glasses tossed on the table like that mean "Sir, this is an outrage! How can you expect me to believe such poppycock?"

Of course, you might want to say "poppycock!" too, just because it's fun to say. Balderdash, maybe.

But you don't really need to. The glasses, properly tossed, will say it even more eloquently than words can.

Now try any of this with contact lenses.

Try to say "poppycock" by knuckling a lens out of your eye. Once you get it out, see whether dashing it to the table makes anyone cringe. I think you get my point.

Contact lenses are just to help you see, and that is fine, as far as it goes. Glasses, however, are not just to help you see. They also help you to be heard.

Has there ever been a TV or movie lawyer who didn't burrow into a cross examination by bouncing the earpiece of his glasses on his chin? Has there ever been a TV surgeon who didn't take off her glasses to evaluate a tricky diagnosis? Or express worry by pointedly removing her glasses and pinching the bridge of her nose?

I've learned recently that other things work, too.

When I was reviewing this principle in the barbershop the other day, a friend told me that, selling cars long ago, he learned the hat trick.

It works this way. You go to a car salesperson and ask for his or her best price. When the salesperson announces the price, just take off your hat. Chances are the price will come down as the hat does.

You can do this only once, though; and it doesn't help to wear multiple hats into the dealership angling for multiple discounts.

Think you could do this with a hood on your jacket? Think you could win an argument with contact lenses?

They ought to teach this stuff in school.

Watching Watches

'Tis with our judgments as our watches: none
Go just alike, yet each believes his own.
                    Alexander Pope, "An Essay on Criticism"

You know the old joke about the fellow whose watch didn't run at all. He liked it that way because whereas most people's watches are always a little wrong, his was right twice a day.

Used to be, you had to wind your watch every morning. Then it ran a little fast or a little slow all day long, and about once a week you reset it to the radio or something. You knew the time, but not precisely. Nobody did, and we got along pretty well. Somewhere there was a standard, an absolutely correct time, but it didn't matter much to anyone's actual life.

That was then. Recently a friend gave me an atomic clock. According to the manufacturer, it radios the Naval Observatory several times a day and resets itself. It tells me the date and time, correct to the hundredth of a second. Even in places like Singapore, as if I cared.

We all know people who set their watches a few minutes fast, so they won't be late to meetings. This always seemed to me like a silly exercise in fooling oneself. People aren't late for things because of the way they attend to time, but instead because they don't attend to time. These people are always late anyway, and if you kid them about being late, they will claim that setting their watches ahead helps them not be even later.

I'm the kind of person who hates to be tardy. I usually get places far too early, just to avoid being late. Then when I get there too early, people look at me compassionately, and I feel dumb. But I can't help it, and I'm probably too old to change.

Thing is, I'd like to be a person for whom precision to the hundredth of a second is important, but I'm really not one of those. Instead, I am the kind of person who needs just a little imprecision. A little tolerance, if you will.

And I think most of us are like that: if it is two or three minutes to nine, instead of exactly nine, then that is OK for most human purposes. If the meeting is for nine o'clock, nobody really expects it to begin just as the great second hand in the sky sweeps across the top of the dial. And more important: we don't *need* the meeting to start that precisely. We manage with a little imprecision.

I think that is probably healthy. After all, measuring time is a human invention. It is nine o'clock because we all agree that it is. We own the time and the time of day. It doesn't own us. Or shouldn't. The time can be whatever we decide.

It's that way about most things, if you think about it. We can pretty much decide among ourselves how we want to live. We make the rules. The rules have to work for us, not the other way around. We don't discover most truths: we invent them.

The person who prefers to wear a broken watch is silly. He thinks time is real and immutable; and he is so afraid of being wrong that he prefers not to know when he is right. All he knows is that if nothing ever changes, he will be safe in some way.

The only reason this guy wears a watch is so he can have something to talk about.

GAMES KIDS AND OTHER PEOPLE PLAY

Games People Could Play If They Wanted To

Recently a reporter interviewed some people, asking what they considered the best game of this century.

Responses were generally predictable: Pokemon, Barbie Dolls, and so on. You expected those answers.

But my favorite response came from a mature gentleman who answered simply: Marbles. I thought that was the most astute answer.

Actually, I'm not certain that marbles are a 20th-century invention. Probably not, but I still like the answer.

I don't think kids play marbles much anymore. When I was a kid, there was a day each spring when we mysteriously knew marbles season began, and on that day, as if by appointment, we came to school with marbles in our pockets.

I'm not just bragging here, but I was pretty good. No, let's be truthful: I was the best. I never lost. A friend who thought he was pretty good used to come to my house afternoons to play. He strode up with a heavy pocket and a light heart, and trudged home in about an hour and a half with the reverse.

We played by rigid, complex rules, with special terminology and a clear set of players' ethics. At some point I read about formal marbles competitions that used other rules, but those rules seemed dumb and boring to me. For a while I thought maybe we didn't know what we were doing playing by our special set of rules, but now I know it wasn't us.

Marbles was fun, cheap, and safe. It rewarded success tangibly: with the other kid's marbles. It taught us valuable lessons in taking turns, playing fair, winning graciously, and, for the other kids, losing cheerfully. The gentleman in the paper was right: it's an excellent game, and I'm sorry we seem to have misplaced it.

I saw a commercial on TV today for another game.

First there were images of huge electronic-looking football players rumbling around on an artificial-looking field. There were the standard TV-style grunts and growls: UUNGHH! HUUUHHH! and so on. Turns out it was an ad for an electronic football game.

Then it showed two boys actually playing the game. These were actors feigning excitement, with a little machine between them about the size and shape of a large soap dish. They were mashing at it with their thumbs as fast as they could. That was it. That was football.

For some reason, they only showed this part of the commercial for maybe two seconds.

If I seem unenthusiastic, it is because I am. Is this what we have replaced marbles with? Jabbing your thumb on a little board so lights will jump around a soap dish? Is this really fun for kids? Or just for game developers and marketers and advertisers?

I don't mean to suggest we ought to scrap electronic toys and replace them with marbles. But I would suggest that parents might help their kids find some of the games we have begun to forget. Many of you know that chess is my game, and I can tell you for a fact that millions of kids find it extremely fun.

And kids like Monopoly, Scrabble, Othello, Clue, checkers, dominoes, and Parcheesi too, for that matter.

These are games that players get wrapped up in, that let players outwit each other, that supply the fun with the play, rather than with artificial lights and commercial grunts.

I think this is what the intelligent gentleman in the paper had in mind. The best games are the ones that get the kids' heads involved.

There is a difference between learning to play, and having people buy toys for you. One of those is actually fun.

A Lesson In Flying

Flying a kite is a three-step procedure.
    First, of course, you have to make the kite. You can make it with yardsticks, string, and newspaper, of course. But that's a serious challenge for littler kids.

It's perfectly all right to buy a kite kit: two sticks united with a little metal loop, some red or green paper, and a length of string. The sticks have little grooves in the ends.

Children of all ages should participate in the kite-making, and if possible, older children should help the younger children. The good thing about kite-making is that adults are as clumsy about it as kids are, so there's very little way they can spoil the fun.

Younger kids won't quite understand the theory of a kite. Why should the sticks bend the wrong way? Why should the string around all the outside corners be stretched so tight? Wouldn't this be easier if it were kind of loose?

Why do you have so much string attached to the kite? Wouldn't it be best just to have one string where the sticks cross, instead of four strings coming from the corners?

Why do you need a tail? It's messy, and besides, a little kid can't quite grasp what the tail of a kite does.

And so on: you have a nice hour or two of stringing, answering questions, gluing, explaining, and tying. At the end of it all you have at least one big red shield-shaped kite, and, I hope, a long long piece of string wound around a stick. So far, so good.

The second step is getting the kite airborne.

Paul Cox

You've selected a site—preferably a big open lot, where there's good straight wind and not many trees. Ordinarily, trees are a blessing, but on kite day they mess up the wind and grab kites out of the air.

Now the adults and big kids have to do the work. Pay out a little line and run into the wind letting the kite drag behind you. Suddenly, if you've paid out the right amount of line and there's a useful breeze, you will feel a jerk as the kite abruptly learns to fly.

It's a little like hooking a big fish: the kite will yank and thrash, try to pull away from you, and then exuberantly climb higher and higher into the sky. It hangs up there in the heavens showing off for everybody, sassy, full of life and snap.

Now the third step: turning the controls over to the little kids.

They will be jumping up and down. "Lemme fly it, Daddy! I got to fly it some!"

So you let them share the string for a minute or two while they get the feel of it. Gradually you let go and pretty soon some little guy no bigger than the kite itself is at the controls.

"Don't let go!" you shout. As an adult you know that the kite can soar only so long as somebody holding the string has both feet solidly on the ground—and you understand the moral implications of that idea.

And you watch as your kid comes to realize something even more important: nobody flies a kite. All we can do is give the kite to the air and try to keep it from crashing into a tree. The kite, like so many of the most interesting things in life, flies itself if we help it a little.

But don't mention any of this. Just as the kite flies itself, so the lessons someday will teach themselves.

Flying kites is just for having fun.

A Verbal Prestige-Enhancement Procedure

I spent some time at Oklahoma University during the tenure of the famous football coach, Bud Wilkinson.

I developed an admiration for Wilkinson. He was a gentleman in a rough sport, and he put high demands on his players.

Believe it or not, kiddies, there was a time when famous college athletes were wholesome people—actual students, and even modest at times. That was the sort of athlete who played for Bud Wilkinson. They weren't thugs, and they attended to their academic work—or washed out.

People respected Wilkinson, and they had good reason to.

So I am sorry to say that Bud Wilkinson is the villain of this piece.

You see, he was a scientific analyst of football. He knew the statistics, knew how to calculate the main chance, knew how many chances he could expect to get, and what was the smart way to use his chances.

But the translation of running, hitting, blocking, tackling, and such into intelligible English doesn't come easy. So when Wilkinson came on TV every Sunday morning, his analysis of yesterday's game often sounded curiously odd and stiff.

"...So unfortunately that resulted in a negative yardage situation for us."

" . . .Resulted in a score-enhancement opportunity which we were able to capitalize on."

"...Can be expected to advance 4.2 yards each and every time he touches the ball."

You get what I'm saying. Most people would have said "We lost on that play," or "We scored," or "He's a strong runner." But Bud said it Bud's way, which sounded formal, analytical, official. Nice guy, but a little stiff in speaking.

He inadvertently created a style of expression that I call TV analytic. Here's how you do it.

Most things you represent using a vague noun like "situation" or "opportunity," and then apply some kind of quantitative-sounding adjectives in front of it. "Negative-yardage situation."

Or you use a slightly vague, ambiguous statistic like "each and every time he touches the ball." Of course, the "each and every" part refers to your expectation, not to the runner's performance. And "each and every" is three words doing the work of one.

But it sounds terrific, when pronounced just so. And you'll hear those same phrases next football season, carefully pronounced by serious people who want to sound advanced. Just wait.

I was thinking of Bud Wilkinson the other night when a TV weather announcer identified a big rainstorm as a "significant *PRE*cip event." A what? "*PRE*cip" means rain, I think. A big rainstorm, did he say?

I seem to recall hearing a weather announcer at some time referring to an "electro-turbulence event" someplace in Kansas. I think that was a thunderstorm, but an "electro-turbulence event" sounds scarier, like something on Jupiter.

I wonder if we can't make our own everyday speech seem more important using these techniques. It's worth a try.

Could a landscaper speak of a spring shower as a "foliation enhancement stimulus event"?

Would a thoughtful dentist administer an "agony minimization introduction" instead of a squirt of xylocaine?

Maybe a baker would slide cake batter into a "thermal-intensive preparation cavity" for 40 minutes or until brown.

Can you imagine an exasperated parent treating the brat to an "intermittent percussive manual application" to his sit-down?

Or threatening a wayward teenager with a "mobility limitation advisement"? It's much less embarrassing to the teenager than grounding.

Maybe instead of bugs or worms we could catch trout with "embarbed faunal attractants." Wouldn't that be more scientific?

Wow, this is fun.

Kind of an "automated column incrementation methodology." I think I like it.

Announcing Xtreme Baseball

Recently scientists have developed an improved strain of football, which is called Xtreme Football.

It's the most newsworthy of a series of "Xtreme" sports with which people amuse themselves these days.

These sports aren't for playing, of course; they're for watching. They are played only by trained professionals. You are warned not to attempt these sports at home.

Xtreme sports appear to have certain common characteristics. Generally they are more violent, more dangerous, and more infantile than the regular sports of which they are derivatives. These observations yield useful guidelines.

In the spirit of Xtreme football and following these guidelines, I offer a proposal to punch up the stodgy old game of traditional baseball.

I propose Xtreme Baseball. Let's call it XB2 just because that sounds edgy and space-agey.

Here's how it will work.

It will improve on regular baseball by using not one pitcher and batter at a time, but at least two. Spectators, you see, like to see action, hits, scoring. Multiple sets of pitchers and batters will therefore be more satisfying for the fans than one.

The pitchers' goals will not be just to frustrate the batters and prevent them from scoring. Not in XB2, where the pitchers' goals are to hit the batters in the heads.

To even things out, the baseballs will be about the size of frying pans, and yellow, so the batters can see them coming and get good swings. Lots of hits, see! Exciting for the fans.

To put an extra twist on this, we'll require the batters to stand back-to-back, one righty and one lefty. They'll have to swing at every pitch! Hey—mayhem! Fun!

Of course, safety is our Primary Concern. Recognizing that the batters might accidentally club one another as they swing, we'll have the batters wear large, bulbous, Day-Glo padded turbans, to reduce the threat of injury.

And give them cards with printed warnings.

Next, we'll improve on this base-running business. That's boring—first base, second base, third base, home again, jiggedy-jig. We can do better than that.

If a batter gets a hit, he must chase the ball so he can hit it again and again until it goes over the fence! Only then does it score points!

The fielders try to beat him to the ball, and if they do, they can put him out by conking him with the ball. Not just a put-out, but a real knock-out!

No foul balls, of course. Runners, several of them at a time, maybe, will be running wild all over the place, in the dugouts, at the concession stands, in the rest-rooms, chasing the ball, dodging throws from the fielders! Running into one another! Maybe there'll be a fight!

It'll be like a barnyard in a hailstorm! Talk about excitement!

How do we score? Well, we know that fans like high-scoring games. Pinball, for instance, attracts a huge following for that reason. So instead of one point for a home run, we'll award a million points! And bonuses if you hit special buttons beyond the fences that make lights flash and buzzers squawk!

Try to picture it! Guys in big lime-colored turbans running all over the place with bats! Flailing away at these big balls! Fielders chasing them, throwing at them! Pitchers trying to knock them down (350,000 points, maybe?)

Music and funny pictures on the scoreboard TV. Mascot chickens running around joking with fans and dancing with players. Nachos the size of beach blankets. Paramedics! Sirens! Flashing lights! Explosions!

Timely pauses for commercials, of course.

Paul Cox

Think this sounds like fun? Hey—wait'll you hear about the cheerleaders!

A Baseball Story

Long ago I played baseball with my friends. We met in warm weather in an empty lot with a backstop and little pits for bases.

We chose up sides and played. We had little equipment, and our games were free form.

The number of innings depended on how fast the yarn leaked out of the ball. There was no catcher, only the chicken wire backstop.

One of our friends was a kid named Jimmy, who was kind of slow. Nice kid, but he had a look of bewilderment about his eyes.

Jimmy loved to play baseball, and was always there.

We knew, however, that he couldn't manage a real position, so we invented one—in the outfield near somebody else.

The somebody else was not to protect that portion of the outfield from Jimmy but to protect Jimmy from the ball.

Because it had been demonstrated repeatedly that Jimmy couldn't catch a flying ball. Just couldn't.

It wasn't that he flinched. He just didn't react at all. He seemed not to believe the ball was real, and would be astonished when it hit him wherever it happened to hit him. If it didn't hurt much, he would then pick the ball up and throw it to somebody. If it did hurt, he would cry.

We created his position, then, so he could play without getting hurt. The other kid called any fly balls. Slow rollers were Jimmy's responsibility. He waited for them, picked them up, and threw them to the infield with visible satisfaction.

He preferred not to bat, and that was good, because he couldn't hold onto a bat after swinging it. It was risky being near when Jimmy tried to bat; you could get hurt.

One summer Little League came to town. All the kids were excited. Somebody assigned us to teams and issued uniforms. Four teams, four combinations of blue or red with white or gray. We had coaches, youngish men with starter paunches, short hair, and whistles. Real baseballs, and real bases.

Before the league schedule began, we put on our uniforms and went to the Little League field at appointed times for practice.

Our coach assigned positions, and I noticed with silent concern that Jimmy was assigned to center field. Did Coach know?

Apparently not, because soon the inevitable happened: while Jimmy slouched in center field, twiddling with a borrowed glove, waving off honeybees, a fly ball headed directly his way.

Now, when you play baseball, you know instantaneously where any batted ball is going. I don't know how you know it, but you do. If you've played baseball, you know what I mean. So everyone realized right away that Jimmy's only hope was to wander randomly off before the ball hit him.

But he didn't. He idled serenely, unaware of what was happening. His hands, including his glove hand, were on his hips; his eyes were far away.

The ball arched through the sky up, up, up and then down, down, down—directly toward Jimmy.

And a miracle happened. The ball missed Jimmy's head and smacked into his glove. It was not that Jimmy caught the ball, although technically he did. Rather, the ball somehow managed to find the glove. He looked around to see what the yelling was about, looked down at his glove a little surprised, found the ball, and threw it to the infield with a delighted grin as his friends cheered.

Coach soon explained to Jimmy that he couldn't use somebody on his team who wouldn't bat.

As for me, I didn't enjoy Little League much. Something about the uniforms, I guess.

Basketball And The Human Condition Explained

I don't know how it works for little girls, but for boys, maturity begins when a basketball bangs directly into your face.

Now, if you've never been there, don't go. It hurts. A basketball is a big, surprisingly hard thing with a distinctly pebbly surface.

You see real basketball players, huge people with hands as large as bed sheets, who casually throw out a hand to catch a pass. The ball just seems to stick to the player's hand for a second, until he flips to a teammate somewhere up in the air.

Looks like a nice little light ball, doesn't it? Not dangerous. But when it collides with a boy's only face, it's just plain hard, heavy, and painful.

It has several similarities to a young boy's head: it's nearly the same size, and it's round. And it's completely hollow.

When this basketball arrives there is sudden darkness and a big SPROING sound that emerges from deep within your skull. Lights somewhere flash violently, and water spurts in all directions from your head: from your eyes, your nose, your mouth.

For a moment you don't remember just where you are, and you don't really care. Your knees are tired for some reason.

So you do what instinct requires. You holler: "Hey! That hurt! Don't throw it to me when I'm not ready!" You may here insert some sentiments that I will omit for reasons of delicacy.

"Well," replies your treacherous friend and teammate, who threw the ball in the first place: "You've got to be ready!"

And suddenly it hits you. Not the ball again, but a realization. Remember the part about flashing lights?

Basketball is not just running around, throwing a ball at a basket, yelling a little, working up a sweat. It is also a matter of keeping your eye on the ball, being prepared for whatever might happen.

You've got teammates to beware of.

The beginning of adulthood: you realize that if you are going to be in the game, you've got to be ready for anything, any time.

So while you ponder this and kindred truths, another misfortune strikes. A kid—probably littler and younger than you, whom you never considered a scoring threat—scoots around you for an easy lay-up.

Well, not that easy, because he's under five feet tall, but you understand the principle I'm getting at.

And once again your teammates holler: "Hey, doofus! Will you wake up over there? Keep your mind on the game!"

They don't know you're dealing with important revelations. And wouldn't care if they did.

You realize that there's a time for philosophizing and a time for thinking, and basketball ain't the time for philosophizing.

(Meanwhile, down the block the girls are also busy doing whatever they do to begin learning how life operates. You've got all that to deal with pretty soon, too.)

These are tough lessons to digest in a single morning, and you don't have much time for digesting, because instantly another eruption requires your urgent attention. It may be another fifty years or so before you get to process all this data in serenity.

And what will you be doing for that fifty years? Trying to stay ready. Trying not to get popped in the face too often. Keeping your mind on the game. Remembering when to think and when to philosophize.

Wondering why you like to watch basketball so much, those big guys handling that ball so easily and gracefully. Wondering where and how it all began.

And keeping an eye on that speedy little kid who's looking to scoot around you.

Competing By and Over The Rules

My understanding wife threw me quite a 60th birthday party, complete with barbecue, a real live string trio (to whom go my thanks and admiration), friends and family from near and far, and of course, a word game on the back porch.

Now, like most word games, this one is interesting enough to be fun in one way and silly enough to be fun in another.

Whenever we play it, we naturally wind up arguing over the rules. That's what you do when you play silly word games.

When my daughter-in-law Vanessa and I were talking about that odd phenomenon this morning, we made an interesting discovery. I pass our findings on to you as a public service.

The discovery was that a major part of the fun of this game was arguing over the rules. The game itself was pleasant enough, but we got much more deeply, emotionally involved in the arguments. More creative. Our arguments were cleverer than our game strategies.

Well, except for Leslie, who doesn't argue much, but who gave inspired clues.

We remember a few points about the game, but we remember the arguments in comprehensive detail. We might have lost the game, but by gum, we stuck it to them on the issue of impermissible homophones!

Anyway, Vanessa and I have speculated that we can generalize this observation to all games: a big part of the fun is generally arguing over the rules.

Think about it. Remember when you were a really little kid? You played games with other kids, none over kindergarten age, and no one was really sure of the rules.

If it was a game that required equipment, you usually didn't have all the equipment, but you went ahead and played anyway.

In case you don't—or would rather not—remember that far back, watch small kids playing sometimes. Nothing much has changed since we did it ourselves. Most of the effort goes into working out the rules—often heatedly.

As we get older, we like the rules to be written, usually in the box top. One player reads the box top to all the others, who are impatient to get started playing. Their plan, I guess, is to play until they need a rule, and then check the box top as they go along.

But the box top, like the Bible, not only tells you the rules, but it also requires interpretation. There are inevitable ambiguities; there are provisions that are hard to understand.

Players are inclined to find in the box top what they want to find.

Besides, what is permissible under rule 1.A is forbidden under rule 5.D. How do you decide which applies? Well, you argue about it, of course. And the arguing is at least half the fun.

You hope.

Now, our discovery is that this principle doesn't apply only to parlor games. Ever notice what people talk about after baseball games? Football games? Right: it's the bad call that cost our team the game.

Not the fact that our base runner was slow or lazy—no, the problem wasn't that, it was that the umpire overlooked where the first baseman's toe was.

Not the fact that our field goal kicker was wide to the right, but instead that the other team's fans were hollering too loud, and our guys' signals got mixed up.

So the argument over the rules is as important as the play. I think it's just basic human nature.

Some people actually wonder why people even bother to play games. Don't they realize that playing games—and arguing over the rules—is pretty much all we do?

Differences in Socksual Perspective

I realized that I had a crisis on my hands. I had said the wrong thing, and now I needed a strategy, quickly.

The socks I wanted to wear this morning were missing. I poked around, and finally unloaded my entire sock drawer to search—no luck.

There were, I realized, three possible explanations.

First, a recent house guest could have stolen my socks. Unlikely, I concluded: he isn't much of a thief; and besides, he already has plenty of socks.

Gentlemen just don't steal one another's socks, you see. A bedrock principle of our culture.

The second possible explanation: I could have left them in Pittsburgh on a recent visit. Again, unlikely, because I think I remember wearing them home.

Third, and likeliest, was the possibility that they had rolled out of the drawer and were hiding in the interior of the cabinetry.

So, lost in thought, I thoughtlessly provoked the crisis: "Foo," I think I said. "The socks I want to wear are probably behind the drawer."

My helpful wife was nearby, and has sleeker arms than mine. She offered to reach behind the drawer. And, sure enough, groped them out.

But this helpful act gave her a moral toehold on a familiar topic between us: "Why don't you clean out that drawer, anyway? You don't need all those socks. Get rid of some of them."

That's the crisis. I had foolishly ceded some interest in my sock drawer.

A sock drawer, you see, means many things to me. Perhaps for other men as well.

It is, obviously, a kind of footwear bank. On laundry day I make deposits, and every morning I make a withdrawal. I like to keep a little running balance, just in case. This is the basic purpose of a sock drawer: to assure us as we sleep that we won't have to worry about how our ankles will be kept colorful and warm next day.

But beyond that, a sock drawer is a little thumbnail sketch of my personality and life history.

My socks, like my personality, tend toward shades of tan and brown. There are big wooly socks for wearing around the house in winter, and thin, austere black socks that I used to wear for business.

Colorful socks for colorful occasions, and a few pairs of Christmas socks that I usually forget to wear in season.

There are socks I like to keep because I wore them when I did something interesting long ago, and I feel loyal to them. Socks with pleasant memories. Socks that I like because they look funny, and others I like because one day I'll need them for something.

My sock drawer is a lumpy collection of footwear friends.

But I find I can't explain this all to my wife, especially early in the morning. I could just mumble, "Well, I like my socks." Pretty lame, I know, but the best I could manage in a hurry. I needed a better strategy than that.

"I should go through those. Several pairs have holes, I'll bet."

Aha!

"All of them have holes," I said.

"Then we ought to get rid of them. Why do you need socks with holes in them? What's the idea?"

"They've got to have at least one hole per sock. How else can you get your feet in?"

"What? That's not what I meant! I meant holes like in the heels!"

And that was it. We weren't talking about socks any longer; we were talking about semantics. I felt I was home free.

Crisis over; strategy in place. It was an interesting morning.

Football Practice

I attended a high school football game recently. Our school won big, and the expected heroes performed the expected heroics.

The team looked excellent. The cheerleaders were hoppy and limber. The fans were appreciative of the play, the victory, the hot dogs. Referees ran around and blew whistles, and the announcer told us what we were seeing with perfect fidelity.

The coaches stalked around the sidelines with clipboards, alternating among moods of satisfaction, exasperation, urgency, and pride.

One coach seemed on the verge of apoplexy about a referee's decision. I thought he was going to get thrown off the field, but the referees were forbearing. And as it turned out, the call he was angry about never mattered anyway.

The band was disciplined, sturdy and lively. I've done that: it isn't easy, if you do it right. As they did.

The grandstands got harder and colder as the night wore on, although the freshmen and sophomore students didn't know that. They were busy milling around in little packs, wearing their caps sideways. I thought they needed warmer shirts, and when they get my age they might agree.

Moms had blankets across their knees and talked with each other about household issues, and dads talked about the same things with their buddies.

I made the accidental acquaintance of a fellow about my age, with whom I compared reactions to the game. We generally agreed.

Paul Cox

I was interested in the cheerleaders for the other team.

They were on the far side of the field, performing their art before a handful of disconsolate fans. Their team was being thoroughly dominated—good kids, I'm sure, but they were just overmatched—so these fans had little to cheer about, as the saying goes.

Nonetheless, their cheerleaders, loyal to their team and loyal to the proposition that cheering is always a good idea, kept up their energetic work.

When our team had the ball, we could hear the cheerleaders on the other side of the field exhorting their team to hold 'em! Hit 'em! DEEE-fense! (As the score mounted against them anyway.)

When their team had the ball, their cheerleaders appropriately changed their theme: GO! Hit that line! All the way! (But they were shut out, I'm afraid.)

Even as the score got longer and the time got shorter, nobody gave up. The spirit was willing, you know, but the flesh . . . .

After the game the players shook hands, the coaches looked busy, the referees looked tired, the cheerleaders calmed down, and the fans, still chatting and laughing, headed for the parking lots. Band members, their hats sideways, lugged their big silver instruments off the field. As I drove home, I listened to the local radio station analyzing the game with statistics.

It was, you see, all very important.

Of course, we all knew, deep down, that it didn't matter particularly who won the game or by what score. We knew about scholarship aspirations and coaching careers, of course. It was important in those ways, but we also knew that the rivers would continue to flow downstream and the sun would continue to rise daily regardless of how the game came out.

Here's what was important about it. We knew that the kids practice hard all week for these games, for the football part, the cheerleading part, and the socializing part.

And then the Friday night game is more practice, this time for life. The game is about trying hard, staying cheerful, looking and being cool.

They wear the jerseys they are born to wear; and their parents and friends watch and generally approve.

Can't beat it.

How To Avoid Losing At Poker

Here's a sure way to win money playing poker: get me into the game.

Actually, this method no longer works, because I have learned my lesson the hard way. I'm a terrible poker player.

There are a few activities, like driving a car and teaching, that everyone thinks he or she is good at. And most of us just aren't.

Playing poker is one of them. I've never talked with anyone who doesn't think he or she is an excellent, downright gifted, poker player.

Men, women, even children—everybody thinks so.

But somebody seems always to lose money playing poker, and that suggests to me that at least some of those people are kidding themselves. Only themselves, by the way.

And I figured out that I was one of those people. I proved it to myself once in a painful, embarrassing way.

I miraculously got a really good hand, right off the deal. A straight flush, as I recall, about Queen-high. Beats almost anything this side of the Mississippi.

So I decided to be cagey and pretend I was bluffing. I tried to look as if I was trying to look as if I had a good hand, if you know what I mean.

Immediately everyone folded. "Cox has a straight flush," Don said. I won maybe four cents holding a hand that should have been worth at least a quarter or two.

Well, because we were really poor, that's why.

Paul Cox

Some time after that I got lured into another regular poker game. The kind where a little group of guys gets together every Tuesday night at somebody's house and plays a couple hands, come on over, it'll be fun, low stakes, lots of laughs, you'll have a good time, whaddaya say. Dealer's choice. Maybe a little beer, hey?

The main inducement, honestly, was that one of the regular players was an orthodontist, and I had young kids at the time. The idea was that this guy was a good poker player and a good orthodontist, and you could save on orthodonture more than you lost on poker.

Why didn't I realize how little sense that made?

I discovered that what they were playing was not poker, as understood by loyal Americans, but some hideous home-grown foolishness involving wild cards, hi-lo pots, goofy betting rules, and special terminology.

You were supposed to "burn threes," and what is worse, to understand what that meant.

You had to keep track of an ever-changing kaleidoscope of wild cards. You had to celebrate incomprehensible events with rounds of betting.

Everybody but me had a great time. And somehow somebody managed to win at this game. The somebody was never me.

There are those, of course, who maintain that all gambling is a sin. I would agree with them that it is a folly, even for some a sickness.

There are those who believe all card-playing is a sin, presumably because some card-playing involves gambling. My father, a Christian minister, didn't bring us up to believe that, although some of his parishioners thought he should have.

As for me, I don't know that "sin" is quite the word I'd apply to gambling, but I don't have strong enough feelings about that to argue the point.

What I do know, from abundant evidence, is that I personally have no talent for it. None whatsoever.

And further, that most people who think they do have such talents are wrong, to the everlasting joy of those few who do.

So I no longer play poker. Ever. Deal me out for good. I folded long ago.

Yessir. You bet.

How To Be A Little Deaf

I have discovered that there are advantages to being a little deaf. You have to learn how to play it, of course.

Here's how I learned to use my little affliction. Several years ago, when I was unused to being a little deaf, my brother and I went to a fast food place to pick up a bucket of chicken for a family gathering. I placed our order, and the child behind the counter said something to me that sounded like, "REEGEX KIPPY?" I tried to be polite, but even after several repetitions, I couldn't figure out what she was saying.

My brother then courteously intervened: "I think she wonders whether we want the original or the extra-crispy recipe." Now all I had to do to close the deal was to look hard at him and say, "What?" Of course, he took over the transaction. And, to get to the point, he got to pay. As we drove home, I realized I had stumbled into something useful.

I decided to learn how to use it. Here are some thoughts.

Being deaf is a terrific excuse when you need an excuse most. Let's imagine that you are talking with someone and you prefer, for whatever reason, to be thinking about something else instead of what the person is saying. Don't tell me you have never been there.

If you have established a reputation for deafness, you can just watch the person talk and think about whatever you like. When you see the person stop, then shake your head ever so slightly and make a wan smile. This means, in gesture language, "Sorry. Didn't hear you. Can't respond." If you do this twice, the conversation is over, and you didn't have to be discourteous.

Paul Cox

See how it works?

Deafness also can provide you with a special panache. You're in a job interview. The person interviewing you is excessively impressed with himself or herself, but so what? You need the job. So you wait for a tiny little opening, and then step over and shut the door. (This doesn't work if the door is already shut.)

Explain that you have a little trouble hearing, and can concentrate better without the ambient noise. That is the key phrase, "ambient noise." It implies that what your interviewer is saying is the very opposite of noise, junk sound. It implies that you really need—and want! —to catch every little syllable of this person's speech. It can score you up to fifteen points on an interview, if done correctly.

What is more, it places you in a vague but benign sort of protectable category. Your interviewer can decide that hiring you will somehow look good to the Feds and also bring somebody into the company that admires what he or she says. More points, see.

The deaf person gets to sit wherever he or she wants to in a restaurant (say something vague about a "bad ear" or a "good ear"), at a concert (same mantra), at a play. The deaf person can politely ask the other person to repeat a statement while he (the deaf person) formulates and polishes a witty response. The deaf person gets to walk past others who seek his or her attention. The deaf person has an excuse to miss church. The deaf person can decide to answer a different question from what was asked, if he or she would prefer to. Who would ask a deaf person to baby sit? Why would a deaf person be expected to attend a rock or C&W concert? If the deaf person is lucky, he or she will sometimes even get to control the TV remote.

And when I'm not paying attention and don't reply to my wife, it's because I didn't hear her.

I Know! Let's Go Camping!

When I was young, I liked to go camping with my friends on autumn weekends. I can't remember just why.

Most of my memories of camping weekends are vague images involving rope, fire, and hatchets. I seem to recall doing very dangerous things with those, and having a lot of fun.

Nobody ever got hurt. I can't explain that part of it.

We planned our camping trips carefully, usually several minutes before Friday afternoon departure. Then we told our folks.

Our mothers quickly became deeply involved in the planning. We needed something to eat, something to cook it in, clean clothes to change into (we did?), hats.

Our plan had been to get out in the woods, go hunting or fishing or something if we could rig a trap or a line, and then cook our catch into a sumptuous banquet. Easy, see?

Our mothers pointed out that we had nothing to hunt with, nothing to fish with, and nothing to cook anything in, like a pot. Or a pan. Well, it was a valid point.

When I realized she was right, my thinking took a sharp turn. I wanted to be elaborately provisioned. I was going to create a culinary miracle in the forest.

The planning degenerated into a contest between kids and mothers, played out in pretty much the same language simultaneously in everyone's home.

My mother was reluctant for me to go into the wild unprepared, but equally reluctant to have me take expensive cookware (this was in the days of S & H Green Stamps). She was somewhat dubious of the whole camping impulse, but indulgent.

The argument ran something like this. My mother noted that my desire to take lots of elaborate equipment was contrary to my original objective of roughing it for the weekend.

My counter-argument was "Aw, Ma!" I relied not on logic but on expressive skill.

Anyway, Mother and I eventually reached some kind of compromise, and we campers set off. We jammed as many kids as possible into a pickup truck (one of the older kids, obviously), and bounced off.

We pitched army-surplus whisky-scented pup tents with wooden pegs and sticks we found, and carefully ditched them. Pulled the ropes as tight as the pegs would allow.

Sleeping bags? Nothing so fancy as that: a couple of army blankets. Toiletries? Gee, we must have forgot.

Then we played, and that's the vague part. It was royal fun: boisterous, strenuous, and of course, hideously dangerous play. It went on until we were thoroughly bushed.

Eventually we cooked and ate. Ground beef, of course, shaped into hamburgers. Some kid always had hot dogs. Warmish pop. Bread and maybe mustard. Nothing fancy, of course: all our mothers were superior rhetoricians.

But nothing ever tasted better.

Then as the fire burned low, we talked. Hair-raisingly lewd jokes. (Nowadays I'm embarrassed even to know such jokes exist.) Terrifying stories. Elaborate insults and counter-insults.

When the fire seemed in danger of going out, we found something to burn and resumed our scandalous, incredibly funny talk.

Eventually we couldn't stay awake any longer. We went into our tents, rolled ourselves up in the army blankets, and slept on the ground. Experienced kids had hollowed out places for shoulders and hips. The rest were too tired to care.

We slept for maybe an hour or two, woke up, and had more fun. Breakfast? Leftover bread and horrible coffee.

Finally, on Sunday afternoon, we climbed into the pickup and jolted home—filthy, exhausted, hungry, and satisfied.

I wish I could remember more about it. Probably best that I can't, though.

The Art Of The Long Game

Generally, when people ask me whether I play golf, I say no, I don't. But it isn't quite true.

Truth is, I'm in the middle of a game. It began around 1960, when a friend offered to show me how to play, and I wanted to see what golf was all about.

We decided to play nine holes at the local course, which may have doubled as a drive-in movie or a gravel pit. But we ran out of time, and had to suspend our game.

Golf, as you know, is played by hitting a tiny slick ball with an ugly stick.

There are several such sticks. The first one you use has a long, spindly, flexible shaft. This flexibility accounts for most of the fun of golf: you can whip the stick around and it will say "WRRP! WRRP!" Like Zorro.

Don't do this, however, when near your opponent, because he or she also has a club. A word to the wise.

Stuck onto the bottom end is a hardened globule of something. It looks to me like a hypodermic needle, when somebody pushes a little of the juice up to get air out. There is this little droplet of fluid perched on the end of the needle, remember? A golf club looks like that.

You're supposed to swing this stick a certain way. You bend one arm, but not the other. I don't think it matters which you bend and which you don't, so long as you bend exactly one.

Paul Cox

You draw the club back until the entire apparatus is wound around your body, and then lurch spasmodically, slinging yourself generally forward.

Now, then. On a little tee before you rests the smiling ball, waiting for you to send it away on a nice trip. It wants to go to the green, which appears to be someplace near Denver.

Your slash the club toward this ball, and one of a few things happens.

You may swing too low, and simply drive the globule of your club into the ground. This disappoints your ball and throws your back out, so it is a bad thing. You are assessed one stroke.

Or you may swing too high, and hit nothing except perhaps yourself. Your first sign that this happened is that your glasses fly off your head and into your opponent's bag. Your friends laugh cheerily, but even so, it's another bad thing. You are assessed a stroke.

The third bad thing is that you might contact the ball.

In this case it squirts off the tee headed east or west, depending on luck, and trickles toward a spiny bush, under which it cowers. You will have to thrash around under the bush for a good while before it emerges. You are assessed maybe twenty-eight strokes.

Incidentally, some players establish a maximum number of strokes per hole; after this number, you may quit that hole, even if the ball is still visible. We did in my game. We set our hole maximum to 65 per player, and that worked pretty well.

Now that you have the ball off the tee, you continue to tease it toward the green using various clubs at random, picking up strokes, penalties, and injuries along the way.

That's how you play golf.

Anyway, I'd like to go back and finish the game I started in 1960. I think my score, for the six holes we completed, is in the middle four hundreds.

I'll just finish this game, see, and then I'll give up golf for good. I'm beginning to get a little tired of it.

The Scooter Phenomenon

When I was young, my friends liked to run around and play. I liked it too—we ran around in empty lots. We hollered a lot, ran a lot, and had a good time.

Sometimes, I suppose, we had an excuse—a ball game, or a game of kick-the-can or tag—but the real point of our running around was just running around.

At some point, though, my friends got scooters.

These, as you will recall, were little red narrow platforms with handlebars on posts and little dinky wheels at either end.

The idea was that you put one foot on the platform and kicked yourself forward with the other.

Now, I didn't see this as a major advance over running. It wasn't particularly fast, and it was just as tiring as running. Maybe more so: we aren't evolved for kicking ourselves along. Of course, as I kid I didn't think of it in those terms, but scooting just never seemed natural.

And most important, a scooter doesn't work well in an empty lot. You have to scoot on a sidewalk. This limits your ability to go in circles, of course, and circles are fun.

I didn't much like scooting, then, but what could I do? People had scooters, so while I prepared to run around an empty lot with my friends, they were rumbling off down the sidewalk on their dumb scooters.

I felt like an idiot running behind. So all I could do was petition for a scooter. My parents—benevolent but not really prosperous—

finally granted my petition. I got a scooter and went outdoors to scoot down the sidewalk with my friends.

Only to discover that I was one development behind. They were disappearing down the street—the *street*, mind you!—on bicycles!

I was flabbergasted. I tried to keep up with my scooter, but again, I felt like an idiot. It was tough: you can imagine.

What could I do? I had just exhausted my credit getting my parents to fund the scooter. I didn't know how I could go back to them: "You know that nice scooter? Thanks, but I'm afraid it's useless." Not an appealing option.

But eventually I had to. I waited as long as I could, scooting down nearby sidewalks alone, trying to persuade myself that I was having a good time.

But I had converted from running to scooting only reluctantly in the first place, and now that the sole justification for the scooter—keeping up with my friends—was gone, I began to hate it. The bicycle was essential.

My father, a kind man, tried to stop the gap by getting an old junked bicycle and painting it up.

But he used white house paint, so the bike looked awful, and besides, it had been junked for a good reason: no human could ride it.

I tried, and eventually even he had to acknowledge that this Moby Bike just wasn't going to serve the purpose.

And finally one Christmas I found a new, blue Shelby bicycle under—well, near—the tree. I learned to ride it that very day, and zoomed off with my friends. Best Christmas gift I ever received.

This part of the story, by the way, has a pleasant ending: I enjoyed the bike for years, and it helped me sustain good childhood friendships.

I note, though, that nowadays scooters are back. Of course, they're silver now, rather than red, and I guess that is much better.

But they're still scooters.

And something in me says: who is trying to kid whom? Know what I mean?

The Tennis Scoring Mystery Explained At Last

People constantly ask me the same question: How do you score the game of tennis?

I can no longer put off explaining it. You may want to sit down.

Bear in mind one fundamental principle: tennis is odd. Repeat this several times before we begin. So, then.

In tennis, you win points to win games, you win games to win sets, and you win sets to win the match.

But you can lose a match even if you score more points and win more games than your opponent. Tennis, remember, is odd.

You win a game by scoring four points. Except that you can't score four points, and you may need to score more than four anyway.

To start, you both have what is called "love." In tennis, as in C&W music, love means nothing.

The first player to win a point gets fifteen points. The second point is also worth fifteen, but the third is worth only ten. Thus, if you and your opponent have each won three points, you are tied forty to forty. Clear?

Only, they don't call it "forty to forty." No, that would make sense. Instead, they call it "deuce." You are said to be "at deuce," which is like "at the dentist's."

You must win a game by at least two points, so from deuce you keep playing until one of you is two points ahead.

But what do these points count? Why, nothing.

If you win the first point after deuce, you have "the advantage." If your opponent wins the next point, you are again "at deuce." The only way you can break this vicious cycle of deuce-advantage is to win two points in a row. From deuce. Still with me?

Theoretically, then, the game could go on forever, with each player winning alternate points. But let's say, for the fun of it, that one of you finally gets the necessary two points ahead. What happens?

You win the game. Does this mean you can stop? Why, not at all: this is tennis.

The first player to win six games wins a set.

But wait: it isn't that simple. What happens if each player has won five games?

Then six isn't enough. So you play two more games. If a player wins both, then he or she wins the set. But if you get tied at six, you can play a tiebreaker, which is a kind of game that nobody understands except one Englishman, and he talks funny.

Unless you're tied at six in the final set. Then it's like deuce, only now it isn't called deuce.

You have to win the final set by at least two games. So you continue to play games—which may or may not feature deuce scores—until somebody gets two games ahead.

The only way to know whether it's the final set is to see whether anybody is in danger of winning.

Among women, the first player to win two sets wins the match, and then they can stop. Among men, you have to win three sets to win the match.

Long ago the tradition was that the winner had to jump over the net. This posed a dilemma: if you exerted enough to win the match, you might be too tired to try the jump without risking serious injury. If not, you might lose, and then where would you be?

So instead, nowadays organizers simply hand the winner a heavy metal object, and he or she is expected to walk around raising this overhead several times while kissing it.

Tennis, as I said, is odd.

Tough Times

You're in a restaurant some time, minding your own business.

Off in a corner of the room you notice a hand bouncing and waving in front of an excited smile. The person waving is vaguely familiar—the kind of acquaintance you might exchange a courteous nod with in the grocery store, but that's about as far as it goes.

However, she's looking directly at you, waving, nearly jumping out of her chair, and grinning to beat the band. Has she just discovered that you are long-lost kin? Did she buy the house next door to you?

Or is the wave for someone else? Yes, that must be it. There's really nothing in your relationship to support such delight.

But you can't be sure of this: she's looking directly at you. What do you do?

Well, you could sit there like a booby, assuming the wave is misdirected. But this is risky: if she really is glad to see you, you don't want to be discourteous. You would be repaying enthusiastic friendliness with cruel disdain—bad business.

You could wave back, trying to match her intensity. But what if she's really waving at someone else? Then you would look foolish, trying to horn in on someone else's fun. In that case, you would earn the disdain—also bad business.

So you try to fashion some kind of innocuous middle course, smiling pleasantly and nodding just a tad. If she's waving at you, you are covered, and can quickly escalate your emotion as needed.

If she's not, then you will just look as if you have been served a plate of hushpuppies.

About that time someone directly between you and the waver jumps up, flails out a responsive counterwave, and cries out. Crisis over; mystery solved. You have been saved from a faux pas—saved, that is, until next time.

My point is simple. Uncertain friendliness is as much a social problem as outright unfriendliness. Maybe even more.

We all know how to handle overt unfriendliness more or less gracefully. We use dignified restraint and let our tormentor hang himself or herself with the rough rope of hostility. These are easy situations to negotiate, and you lose face only if you show that you are bothered.

The difficult occasions arise not from unambiguous unfriendliness, but from ambiguous friendliness. Got that?

From the hostess who brings you a cup of special, expensive coffee you can't drink, and then looks hurt when you don't drink it. Should you drink the coffee and live with the heebie-jeebies the rest of the evening, or instead incur the reprehension due to an ingrate?

From the friend who wants to take you out on his sailboat. You make some kind of transparent excuse such as that you're sorry, all you have is leather shoes. The jovial friend offers you some ratty boating shoes, and you are suddenly in deeper than ever.

From the relative who gives you what he or she incorrectly thinks is a pretty tie for Christmas, and then invites you to church. Do you wear this tie to please the donor, outraging the rest of civilization? Well, of course you do, suffering the whole time.

Of course, none of these people would ever really do anything to make you uncomfortable. They're just being nice. You've got to be happy about that.

It's a privilege to live among people who are cheerful and generous. We are all thankful about it.

But if you tell me you don't sometimes find that pleasantness complicates your life just a bit, I'm not going to believe you. Not for a minute.

Two Marriage Strategies That Work

Often columnists give strategies for successful marriage. These include novelties such as fairness, mutual respect, and daily expressions of affection.

They sound good, but there are two tried and true strategies that I want to remind you of: Mutual Concession and Marital Zugswang. These actually work.

The first is Mutual Concession. "Well, Dear, what do you want?" "Oh, I don't know, Honey. What would *you* like?"

Here's a scenario. The wife and husband go to the movie rental place to select their Saturday night entertainment. (You will have noticed already that these people have been married a long time.)

The husband leans toward movies featuring violence, car chases, and raciness. The wife likes tender stories, probing psychology, and emotional honesty. These would be their choices if they were alone. But they are not alone.

The husband selects a movie box with pastel colors featuring women whose faces are thoughtful and whose eyes are misty. "How about this one, Honey?" he says, his tone between enthusiastic and listless. "Siskel liked it."

"Well, maybe. Or we could get this one," she cautiously replies. She's holding a box with a picture of an explosion from which the debris is narrowly missing a man and woman with hypertrophied physical features and torn clothing, who grip bulky pistols in one hand and one another in the other.

These are meaningless exchanges, intended to establish the outer boundaries of choice. They eventually settle on something neither of them quite likes. Mutual Concession.

And that is actually good, because whereas it would have been impossible for them to be equally satisfied, now at least they are equally dissatisfied. The equality, see, is more important than the satisfaction.

The next strategy, Marital Zugswang, borrows its name from chess. Zugswang literally means "move anguish": a condition where you have to move—you can't pass in chess—but any move you make loses. Your opponent is not directly threatening anything, but is instead waiting to pounce no matter where you turn.

Under this paradigm, each spouse creates situations where he or she is not attacking in any real way, but the opponent spouse is nonetheless backed into such a corner that any move is bad. It is what some spouses, in pop-psychological moments, call "passive-aggressive behavior."

Let's extend the scenario. Imagine our couple is now at home on Saturday night with their movie. They start watching it, and sure enough, neither of them really likes it.

The crisis comes when one of the spouses suddenly becomes aware that the other is snoring. Could be either one, but let's assume she's asleep just to keep the pronouns simple.

Does he awaken her? Bad mistake: he would both disturb her nap and disclose that her Mutual Concession ruse had broken down.

Does he let her sleep? Bad mistake: sooner or later she will wake up and wonder aloud why he had rudely finished the movie and turned in, leaving her on the sofa.

Does he open a book to read? Bad mistake: he would be showing that his disdain for her movie choice was only an act, and that he is actually hostile toward the movie. (They both are hostile toward it, but they played the game of Mutual Concession, where you have to pretend enthusiasm.)

See? There is no move that doesn't lose. Marital Zugswang.

Many marriages are, I believe, life-long exercises in Mutual Concession and Marital Zugswang. I believe these work because they are hard strategies to execute. They require careful footwork and delicate maneuvering. They keep us engaged with one another. We're too busy to get bored.

Winning at Conversation

In conversation, as in any other game, your objective is to win. Don't forget it.

To win a conversation means that you establish the upper hand. You get to decide what will be talked about, and your views have the presumption of correctness. The loser in a conversation goes home feeling vaguely dissatisfied and sleeps poorly. The winner sleeps well and makes a lot of money the next day.

Here are some tips to winning conversation.

First, you have to establish ground rules that favor you. Never let the other person decide what you will talk about. Imagine your opponent says something like, "Did you hear that Joanna had a baby?"

This is a pretty good topic, but you didn't bring it up. So you have to wrench the conversation around to something else. You need to do it subtly, because discourtesy is a foul, potentially disqualifying.

"Well, I never expected she would have a color TV," would be rude and dumb. You won't make the final four like that. Even worse would be: "No, I didn't hear that. Did somebody say it?"

"That's three for them now, isn't it?" is a good reply. It gets the conversation away from babies and into either history or mathematics, wherever you feel most superior. "Never cared for babies, myself," is risky, but you can try it.

Second, you should be prepared to change the rules at any moment. Let's say your opponent replies, "Yes, and finally they have a little girl."

You say, "Is she like a melody?" This should work. By suddenly alluding to an old popular song, you throw your opponent completely off the scent. She (I'm assuming here) will get a blank expression, unable to figure out what you are talking about. Don't help by humming the tune.

Your opponent will smile oddly and say, "A melody?" You reply: "Oh, well. Anyway, I understand there's a fortune to be made in Internet investments. You heard about Ted?"

Third, where you look is very important. Some people believe in looking at the other person's ear, but this is obvious and borderline rude.

Where you look depends on the sex of your opponent. If you are talking with a man, the practice is that the speaker looks away and the listener looks at the speaker. I don't know why, but that is the rule. So when he speaks, look at his forehead. When you speak, look at his shoes. Occasionally adopt a puzzled frown, as if there is something wrong with his shoe. Don't mention anything, though.

If your opponent is a woman, you may look at her as you speak. Switch your gaze back and forth between her eyes: left, right, left, right. Not too fast, or she will think you are crazy. Just the right pace, and she will think she's crazy. You should win easily.

Finally, you have to have skill at defense. Sometimes you will be trumped when you least expect it: "Did you hear that Sid might not be the father of Joanna's baby?" This is hard to reply to. You need something to keep you afloat.

Now, kids have a stock response: "Oh, yeah?" But this is weak, because there is an answer: "Yeah." When you are conversing with adults you need better.

Here it is. All you say is "What."

Not "What?" Not "WHA-A-AT!!" Nothing like those, because they award the point to your opponent. Instead you say "What," perfectly flat, no upward or downward inflection, no nothing. Just the one word, with a completely blank face: "What."

Try it tonight on your spouse. If you can win at home, you can win anywhere.

LESSONS

The Lesson of Pinball

You start a game of pinball by shooting a steel ball with a little spring-loaded trigger. The ball rolls up a chute, and then begins a bothered drift down.

It bumps into things—flippers, paddles, railings, contact points. When it hits something, lights flash, bells ring, and a sound-effects chip hollers WYOINNNNG! or something like that. The ball, never that comfortable to begin with, flies off and starts its fall all over.

The person who put in the quarter (or whatever it costs these days) tries to keep the ball alive—in transit and jumping around, that is—by hitting buttons to flip flippers, or bumping the machine, or whatever.

If the player is skillful, the ball keeps flying around. It goes into frenzies bouncing between paddles, swooping over contact points. Sometimes it gets caught between two equally repellant points and just jitters back and forth.

Much as the ball seems to think it is doing something, the game is not actually about the ball. It is instead about gravity. The player has to be constantly on his or her toes to thwart the effect of gravity, which is patiently, tirelessly trying to settle the ball into a little hole.

And eventually gravity succeeds. No player, however good, can keep that ball rolling forever: sooner or later it sinks into its hole with a little plop. Usually the player gets another steel ball, though, so there's no great tragedy. (Or is it the same ball again? I never really knew.)

Pinball is also about points, celebrated by lights and annoying noises. Grim-looking players score hundreds, thousands, even millions of points by keeping the ball out of the hole. The best get their nicknames and top scores posted: WILDMAN 3,716,442.

It's the ultimate contest, then: gravity on one side; points, plus some vanity, on the other.

The poor ball is worked on by both sides, getting knocked about, scoring points for somebody else, in a constant frenzy between scoring points and following gravity to a resting place.

Actually, I never played pinball much. A few times, when I was young. But I had more important things to do, I thought.

It seemed to me that the people who played pinball a lot, who got proficient enough to score in the millions of points—these people maybe needed something useful in their lives.

Besides, now that I'm older, I doubt I could really succeed at pinball. It requires sharp reflexes, quick and subtle motions of the hands and fingers. You have to be able to bump the table hard enough to do some good, but not so hard that the TILT sign goes on.

I probably won't take it up. I really don't think I've got what it takes any longer.

And I'm less interested, too, in scoring millions of points. So I'll let pinball pass me by.

Besides, I'm not sure I want to study the lesson of pinball these days.

At some point you know that most of the flippers have flipped, most of the paddles have paddled, and most of the contact points won't light up many more times. The ball is somehow less interesting, and it trickles down a little more gracefully.

Sometimes it works its way to the hole at the bottom before you are quite ready to react.

See what I mean? Pinball is fine while you're making contact, keeping the ball alive. Racking up points, making the noises zing out and the lights flash. Maybe getting your initials up in lights.

But it's just points, after all, and someday gravity is going to win.

The Guy Who Smelled As A Dog

I read about a fellow who took a serious whack to his head. The whack apparently jostled some connections, because afterwards his sense of smell became sharper. He said he smelled as a dog (not "like" a dog, notice), and his whole world suddenly changed.

He could smell everything. Everywhere he went he smelled the history of the place: all the people who had been there and what they were eating, all the animals, the weather, the litter and whatever happened to be around. He recognized people by their smells, and knew where they had been and what they had been doing.

It was a completely new, exciting world for this man. His enhanced sense of smell allowed him to know things that were hidden from him before. He lived in a more complicated world than you and I do, full of fascinating information. He could smell stories everywhere he went. (If what I read is true, that is.)

As I recall, this blow to his head also cost him some faculties. Probably something involving fractions or long division or maybe irregular verbs. Maybe his world wasn't more complicated, then, but just complicated in a different, more pleasurable way.

A couple of years later the man suffered a kind of counter-whack, perhaps to the other side of his head, which reversed the original whack. He suddenly lost this ability to smell everything.

He became depressed. Said that the ability to smell as a dog smells was so wonderful that if he couldn't have it any longer, he just didn't much want to live. He said he envied dogs, who clearly lead much better lives than people do.

Makes you think.

We humans seem skittish about smells. We don't smell well (or, in some cases, very good, either), and we seem determined to ruin what little sense of smell we have.

Consider what we do. Just in the US, we spend fortunes on perfumes, scented soaps, deodorants, anti-perspirants, and little cardboard pine trees that we hang off the rear view mirror. We buy scented candles, scented hankies to throw in the clothes dryer, and even little doodads you can plug into an electrical outlet to release "floral bouquet" or "spring shower" into the room.

When it comes time to sell your house, you can even buy an aerosol spray that makes the kitchen smell like bread baking.

I had a friend who sloshed perfume on throughout the day, thinking her morning dose had faded. By quitting time she had nowhere to hide—anywhere in the building. You know people who do that, too, I expect.

My point is that we seem obsessed with our feeble sense of smell, always taking odors out or putting them in or changing them. Never quite sure what to do with them.

It's not that we don't care. Barbecue cooking, bread baking, flowers, pine needles—everybody loves these aromas. And we respond powerfully to bad smells. So powerfully that I'm not even going to mention them.

Who was it that said he was reading Spinoza while his neighbor cooked cabbage, and now he can't eat cabbage without thinking of Spinoza? Smells tend to take on odd associations and never to let them go.

This intrigues me. It's as if we humans have just enough sense of smell to realize that we're missing something. Something that every basset hound and rat terrier takes for granted. Something that, if we had it, we might not want to think so much about arithmetic and philosophy and art and commerce and space travel and the Internet.

As I said, it makes you think.

A Lesson About Gardening

My gardening self-confidence suffered a serious blow long ago.

I had been enlisted to help with the garden. My assignment was to pull up all the weeds, on the promise of gingerbread.

Naively I asked: "Which ones are weeds?"

This question earned me a hard look, not so much of reproof as of incredulity. How could anyone not know which were weeds and which were flowers?

"This one," my mother replied, knuckling a straggly thing out of the earth, and leaving me, as they say, still on square one.

I tried to understand the lesson she intended to teach, but I couldn't. "Is this a weed?" I asked of some equally straggly looking thing. It was not, but little further information came.

Finally, after I had asked several times, my mother gave me a rule: "A weed is just anything that looks like it doesn't belong. Leave the rest alone."

You can guess what happened. I uprooted what didn't have blossoms and left what did. I grubbed up flowers that hadn't bloomed yet, leaving the bright yellow dandelions.

This time the look was sterner, a bit more reproving, and I was judged not to merit gingerbread.

I remain about as ignorant of flowers and weeds now as then. People are amazed. When it is time for gardening, I like to find some urgent chore just to avoid having to come to terms with my inadequacy.

But I've discovered that gardening is not just about knowing flowers and weeds (thank goodness). Let me explain.

The definition of what is a weed and what is not is just a bit arbitrary, after all. And people's tastes differ.

Generally, it seems, the definition of what is a flower and what is a weed is determined by whose garden it is. Within ones own garden, ones decree is infallible.

There are some common agreements, of course. Everyone pretty much agrees on crabgrass, for instance (a weed, I believe). But otherwise our gardens are our own worlds to make.

Not always alone, though, and that is the interesting part. Sovereignty over a garden can be shared.

You may have noticed that many couples garden together. They go out on pleasant weekends and dig around in the dirt, haul mulch, pull weeds without consultation, get loam under their fingernails, and somehow make a garden together.

How do they do that? How do they come to know each other's definition of a weed? Of a flower? Where is the jointly held plan they are working from? Whose head holds the blueprint?

Of course, there isn't any.

Some couples just are so closely tuned to each other that they appear automatically to know what kind of garden they are building together. They agree without discussion, probably without knowing that agreement is happening.

They just do what comes naturally, and a coherent garden results.

Out of a patch of nondescript ground, they are able to unite the creating energy of nature with the discipline of human judgment, and make their little piece of world finer.

The miracle isn't just that flowers are beautiful. It is also miraculous that people understand each other well enough to agree on what "beautiful" is.

And that's what I mean when I say gardening is not just about flowers and weeds. It's becoming part of another person or group so fully that you don't need to check. Cultivating more than just flowers and weeds. Growing homes, families, circles of friends, and communities.

All you need for that is to be human. And some hard work.

What's more important in life than creating gardens together?

Dilemmas Involving Portraits and Ceiling Fans

Two subjects came up recently that seem to have a lot in common, if your squint your eyes just right.

The first appeared in an anguished letter to one of the prominent advice columnists—I don't remember which sister is which, nor do I think there is any difference between them worth remembering.

In this matter, the letter-writer asked the columnist whether it was all right to have a picture of an ex-husband in her living room. She said she and the ex-husband were amicable, and had shared some important and pleasant life history. So is it proper for her to have the picture displayed on a living-room wall?

The answer, which I am summarizing, was: if you want to, yes. Why not?

I thought that one was easy, but it seemed to me odd that the writer should even have felt the need to ask. It's her picture, and her living room. Why did she need permission from an advice columnist?

The second issue had to so with those overhead fans that people have in various rooms of the house. You can choose the direction in which they spin, and the question was: should the fan blow upward in summer and downward in winter—or the other way around?

This conversation ranged over many variables. The height of the ceiling. The immediate physical sensation of a breeze cooling the skin by evaporation. The difference between temperature and the sensation of comfort. How many people were in the room, and where they were located relative to the fan. Probably several others.

Paul Cox

And we finally ended the topic with a suggestion by one of the participants, who holds a Ph. D. in Nuclear Science and Engineering. It was this: get a floor fan.

This was not the first time I have heard this topic debated, and I'm fascinated by the depth of conviction and the height of passion it seems to excite. By the subtleties of analysis it provokes. By the wealth of life experience that is showered on it.

I have a friend who is either an up-draft or a down-draft partisan—for one season or the other—but I can never remember which. It seems to mean a lot to him, so I'm a little afraid to invite him over.

He doesn't like my politics much, and I'm concerned that if I add the outrage of a fan error, I'll be in serious trouble.

My stance on the fan issue, you see, is like my stance on the portrait issue: when it's your fan and your house, why ask? What does it matter?

That seems to satisfy my interest in both subjects. They are subjects I don't really care much about, so I can't see why anyone else does.

But maybe that's a little too glib. Maybe I need to re-think. After all, different things matter to different people. Is it my place to tell people what they should feel strongly about?

So I have to modify my position a little, like this: When it's your picture, your fan, your house, then who am I to say it doesn't matter?

If something matters to you, then it matters. If it doesn't matter to me, but it does matter to you, then it matters.

And the other way around: don't expect me to get passionate about your issue, so long as it is just your own private issue. I'll promise not to belittle your convictions by saying they don't matter.

After all, none of us is going to have enough time here to waste quibbling over what to quibble over.

How Spiders Shout

I figured out how spiders shout. Let me explain.

We were living on the 49th floor of a Chicago high-rise. Pretty much the entire outside wall of the apartment was window.

Oddly, colonies of spiders settled on the outsides of the windows every summer.

What were they doing there? I'm not sure, but I think they lived on the gnats and mayflies that were lofted up there on the wind.

In early summer there were only a few little spiders. But as these succeeded, they grew bigger, and set up large webs, where they caught flying bugs. The more they ate, the more they needed.

As they succeeded, they multiplied. Our small colony of little spiders became a big colony of large spiders, and this was the problem. There was only a fixed amount of window space and food, but an increasing number of webs of increasing size.

This meant that the spiders had to compete.

Now, we have all read about the gemlike beauty, symmetry, and serenity of lovely garden spiders.

Not these guys. They lived in tattered, messy webs littered with the carcasses of recent lunches. They never neatened up. I think they must be nearsighted, because they have to focus on a wispy web and not be bothered by what is going on 49 floors below them.

Their lives, moreover, were ceaseless fighting. Spiders who walked around the web to see what they might have caught inevitably blundered into the neighbor's web, because the webs overlapped. This would wake up the neighbor, who would come running.

Here's where the shouting occurred. The spiders—hideous looking things—would square off. Then one of them would reach down with a front leg and pluck the web. The web would vibrate up and down, vibrating the spiders with it. The other one might pluck back, or else just run away.

The bigger the pluck, the more dangerous the spider.

As the competition got fiercer they ran away less often, and instead closed on each other. They would tear at each other with their legs until one ran off or was injured. The injured spider would curl up in a ball and lie still, sometimes for hours, until the winner walked away.

This plucking, I believe, is the way spiders shout. It's the same way lions—and people—shout: we make the biggest possible vibration in a medium, and the other party perceives the vibration. What seems like a silent pluck to us probably "sounds" like a pretty impressive roar to a spider.

I don't know why I found these spiders so fascinating. They were filthy, violent, and shortsighted. Their lives were nasty, mean, brutish, and short. All they did was eat, fight, and sleep; and the more they succeeded, the more vulnerable they became.

I watched them often. I doubt they watched me, though: too nearsighted.

Finally came the inevitable calamity: window-washing day. Splash, swipe: and whole colonies wound up in disgusting soggy piles of dying arachnids 49 floors below. The building staff hosed them away.

Of course, the spiders' lives illustrate the old retail cliché about location and floor space.

But I think there is a more important lesson. A nearsighted creature that lives only to get his and fight his neighbors has no life. Certainly not a life I want.

We humans don't have to be like spiders. We can see further. We can decide to do more than just eat, fight, make bigger webs, and die.

We are smarter than spiders. And if we choose to be, we can be wiser, too.

The Project That Wouldn't Fly

My first Project Manager assignment came when I was seven. The rest of the project team was between four and six.

One kid had discovered some scrap lumber, a big cardboard refrigerator box, and kindred stuff in his backyard. Looking back, I expect his father had "accidentally" left it there just as summer vacation started.

Anyway, this kid assembled his buddies to decide what to make of it. I was on hand, since I lived just across the street. We decided to make an airplane.

Not a toy airplane, either, but a real one that we could fly to Europe in. We would build the plane and then take a grand trip.

We didn't reach this decision carelessly, either. No, it was the product of a study of the available materials and of our knowledge of airplanes.

"See this here? This can be a wing!"

"We can make the middle part out of this stuff here!"

"This can be that little wingy in the back, with the rudder sticking up!"

So we set to work. My responsibility was to set the tasks and, in general, make certain that we made an airplane rather than something else. It can happen, you know.

We worked for several days, and as we continued, I began to worry.

Here's why. My staff continued to think we were building an airplane. But I developed doubts. Principally I doubted that we would solve the problem of where to sit.

And of how we would get it to hold together.

All we had, remember, was sticks and cardboard. No nails, no tools, nothing like that. What parent would want six-year-olds playing with hammers and nails under the supervision of a seven-year-old?

Workdays were uniformly unproductive. There was big talk about the finished plane we would soon have, and very little actual building. (Or "making" as we called it.)

That is, I would instruct a pair of workers to affix the wing to the fuselage (or "middle part") at the beginning of the workday, and by afternoon, all they had achieved, besides big talk, was to move the wing somewhere.

Eventually I began to see that our project was doomed, but my staff continued in their optimism to lay plans for the trip to Europe. They planned to buy bubble-gum, as I recall.

So I came to work each morning with an increasing sense of dread. It wasn't going to turn out well.

I thought: OK, we won't end up with a plane. But the little kids are having fun, and I can just go along with it and help them have their fun.

And they did have grand fun, too, until the worst happened: big kids came around.

These big kids understood engineering principles, aviation, geography, and physics. They were nine, ten years old—far smarter, wiser, more experienced than anyone on my team. You can guess what they said.

"An airplane? What airplane? Where you going to put the engine, huh?"

"How's your airplane going to fly with no propeller?"

"You can't get anybody inside that thing!"

Of course, they were right. I knew it (although I loyally tried to defend our work). The other kids knew it. We all knew it. We felt downright childish, and you don't want to feel childish around ten-year-olds.

Naturally, all the little kids were upset—with me. Their resentment was ferocious and unqualified. They felt I had led them down a path to foolishness, made them look bad in the eyes of superior kids.

I was the villain. The ultimate failure.
It was, in other words, your typical project.

Thoughts on Toast Management and Injustice

Others have observed what appears to be a rule of life: a dropped piece of toast always lands jelly-side down.

I read a short piece in *Scientific American* a few years ago by a physicist who had studied why. He considered the usual height from which toast falls (roughly 35 inches, I believe) and the number of flips at a standard flip rate that would make the jelly hit the carpet first.

He also took into account the gravitational fructose increment, which is to say that the jelly side is heavier.

And eventually concluded—wisely, I think—that toast falls jelly-side down because life is designed to be annoying. Something about the wisdom of holding onto your toast, as I recall.

Now, it's not the jelly-down issue that I'm concerned with, but the overall system of justice in the universe. I believe it is subtly biased against humans. And we should be glad it is.

Consider, for instance. Last week I saw a squirrel calibrate and execute a spectacular leap. From just the right spot, he hurled himself against a downspout, bounced off onto the *GUARANTEED SQUIRREL-PROOF* baffle on the bird feeder, and then popped up onto the feeder. Clever wretch managed, that is, to convert the baffle into an access route.

Now, this stunt took imagination. He didn't read it in a book, nor on the ironclad warranty we got with the *GUARANTEED SQUIRREL-PROOF* baffle. He had to think the mission up, calculate that it would work, and then have the courage, strength, and agility to pull it off.

Did he do this to cheat us? Nah. He did it to get something to eat. Can't fault him for that.

Did the vendors of this GUARANTEED SQUIRREL-PROOF baffle cheat us? Nah. You can't blame them for failing to anticipate such a stunt (although you might quibble with the boldness of their guarantee).

No. What happened here is that my optimistic wife and I thought we could beat nature by buying the baffle, and we got proven wrong.

Just when you think you've got life whipped, the jelly hits the shag.

So there is a universal people-humbler principle that we need to live with. OK, I can accept that. Why, though, should we be glad of it?

Well, because it keeps us going.

Suppose GUARANTEED SQUIRREL-PROOF baffles actually worked, every time, everywhere. Then what would happen? All the other baffle-makers would themselves be baffled. Out of business, on the dole. All squirrels would slink off in defeat and scratch out a diet of acorns.

Bird-feeding humans, baffle-makers, and squirrels would all become lethargic, lose interest, quit trying.

For an analogy, consider the gadget play in football. I mean any play with unexpected razzle-dazzle, precarious ball handling, and some little magic of deception. The defenders tackle goalposts and one another while the least likely member of the offensive team strolls smiling across the goal line with the ball and winks at his girlfriend in the stands.

What if gadget plays always worked? Boring, right? We would have to switch our attention to another sport, like synchronized arena team squash or the like. Help.

Given a vote, we would opt instead to keep the people-humbler principle.

And in fairness, I should note that the squirrel's attack on the baffle comprised dozens of failing stratagems before he hit pay dirt. I believe he learned from each of his failures.

I don't mind the little people-humblers of life. I really don't. They keep our vanity—and laziness—under control.

Paul Cox

It's just that sooner or later I get really tired of worrying about toast management.

Some Thoughts About Stones

I was in a car somewhere in rural New Jersey (yes, there is a rural New Jersey, and it's really quite pretty), when we passed an old graveyard. The driver said she had visited this graveyard, and seen gravestones from the middle 1600's.

It made me think. The cemetery was on a gentle green slope, surrounded by fields and trees. The stones, weathered and smoothed like the bodies of an elderly congregation, shone silently under the late summer sun.

It was a quiet, graceful scene. Geese, like attendants, flew overhead in solemn, processional formation, obeying the call of the changing seasons as they always have. Everything was in perfect order; nothing needed to be done there.

These stones really are the people whose graves they mark, I thought.

The words and dates have probably washed from them in years of rain and wind, and their descendents are probably scattered all around the country, all around the world.

Nobody remembers these people any longer. Even those who know what their names were, and where they are buried, don't really remember them.

The memories of their descendents are not memories of people, but knowledge of abstract information about people.

It doesn't really much matter, though, about the words and dates, or the shapes of their faces, or the sounds of their footfalls. All that matters is what the clean stones now say: just that these people were here.

Paul Cox

The people in these graves are as anonymous now as their gravestones are illegible. The business of their lives has long ago faded away. All their quarrels are settled by time, all their worries are relieved, their debts forgiven.

All that matters—all that ever mattered, I suppose—is that they were here, and that they are, in some way, still here.

The country they gave birth to is still here, though they couldn't have predicted it. Communities that formed when these people lived near their neighbors, cooperated with them, traded with them, loved them, competed with them—these communities now survive as great modern stone cities, crackling with life.

They wouldn't be recognizable to their ancient founders, any more than they would recognize the founders, but the cities are nonetheless the offspring of their founders' villages.

For most of the history of humankind, stones have been ranked at the bottom of creation. They can't move, they can't think, and, so far as anybody knows, they have no awareness that they even exist.

So humans have always decided that stones lay at the bottom of the visible creation, with ourselves, of course, at the top.

But I think on some level we know that stones and people are mysteriously kin.

We have always found similarities between ourselves and stones—we honor Stonewall Jackson, Saint Peter, and the Rolling Stones. We celebrate our heroes by idealizing them in stone statues.

We carve our most precious memorials in stone. We found our cities and highways on stone, and we pledge love with exquisitely carved, luminous gemstones.

Images in stone are what we build, what our lives create. We carve the stones, and the stones become us. The statue comes to life—the Commendatore avenges himself on Don Giovanni.

We teach stones how to reflect our thoughts, our ideals, our ambitions. We shape stones to tell our stories, to record our ideas—and they shape us, too.

Stones teach us that just being here is more important than most other things.

Life, unlike stone, is always moving and always changing. Stones reveal the power to be found in patience, in stillness, in being put to good use.

What Mosquitoes Mean

When I was young, people sat on the front porch evenings and talked.

A common subject of conversation was why the Almighty had put various things on earth.

The assumption underlying these speculations was that everything was created for us humans: for our help, our edification, our amusement, or the like.

Little attention was wasted on the obvious. Hogs, for instance, were for barbecue, cows for milk and steaks, chickens to fry for the preacher.

Dogs were clearly put here to be fun for kids and husbands, and to help us hunt. Cats were pretty much the same: entertain kids and wives, and control the mice.

But why should there be mice?

This, you see, was trickier. To decide that mice had no particular benefit for humankind was to suggest implicitly that there was a miscalculation in the way the universe was set up.

And further, to make the justification for kitty somewhat shaky.

So the presence of things like mice—extend it to roaches and tigers if you like—required considerable subtlety.

Sometimes the conclusion was simply: those are here for us to exercise our appreciative and analytic skills upon. Or even easier: they are here for reasons beyond our understanding.

It was like looking under the hood of the car. We generally knew the motor was there to make the thing go, but we couldn't readily identify the functions of all the little gears, springs, hoses, and gadgets that went into it.

Well, the red-haired kid two doors down could, but we thought he was making it up most of the time.

This being a summertime, front-porch kind of activity, the list of puzzling species usually came down to mosquitoes. "Well, what do you suppose [slap!] He put these darned [slap!] things here for?"

"Why, I suspect it was to teach us patience, dear."

"Patience? By driving us batty? And they spread malaria! You're going to have to do better than that!"

There the conversation usually foundered, and smaller kids like me fell asleep. We woke the next morning refreshed but welted with red bites.

Nowadays we don't have that conversation much, and I think we are better off.

In the first place, we watch TV instead of sitting on the porch. And when we talk, we talk about Christina Applegate or the Braves, not the divine plan as respects mosquitoes and vermin.

Moreover, I think most of us realize now that maybe the rest of creation isn't here as our tool or our toy. We realize that mosquitoes—and mice and roaches and tigers—are here just because there is a place in the survival scheme for them.

Natural selection, the engine of evolution, has rewarded their adaptations to their surroundings, just as it has given us hands to slap them with. (Not tigers, of course.)

I think we are better off because we don't presume to grade the creation, to decide whether mice and mosquitoes and all "ought" to exist. To evaluate everything by our own tastes or needs. Who did we think we were, anyway?

I think that, in a way, we were insulting the very one whom we were analyzing: claiming the right to judge how the world was made.

Our task is to live in this interesting world, to enjoy it wisely, to help each other where we can, and to leave things as good as we can for our kids.

I do miss sitting on the front porch and talking, though. Baseball might be a good subject to switch to.

Some Thoughts on Peanuts and Order

Recently my energetic wife and I experienced a terrible ordeal: we cleaned up after some remodeling, and this cleaning involved a storage room.

From this experience I took two grim lessons that I'll share with you.

First, I learned that most of our treasures were in a form I little expected: artificial peanuts. I mean the little plugs of hard foam that we use for packing.

These peanuts exist to allow us to pack any old thing, however brittle, in any old box. No need to find just the right size box. Just pour in a layer of peanuts, put in the thing, and fill with peanuts. You can pack a wristwatch in a coffin if you want to: no problem. (Assuming you have a spare coffin handy.)

These peanuts mean we don't have to store up newspapers all through the months of October or November, and then ball the pages up to fill December's gift packages. They also mean that gift recipients in distant cities can't read the news of our high school football team as they open their gifts. Too bad.

We appear somehow to have accumulated many many peanuts. Most of what we had stored was peanuts: huge cartons of them, plastic bags of them.

Before you say anything, look at your own storage room. See?

These peanuts are hard to throw away. You try to consolidate them into fewer containers, but they have quirky ways of sticking to your hands, and finding methods to escape the desired recipient container. So you invariably wind up chasing little puffs of silicon around, and then trying to brush them off your hands.

I'm waddling around like a Christmas goose, wheezing, plucking these stupid things and then unable to put them down.

I'd rather herd roaches into a fire.

Now we have discarded those useless peanuts, and for some reason I feel insecure. I'm afraid of what will happen in December. Probably I'll wind up paying to replace the peanuts. I'll buy too many, of course, and then receive cubic yards of them in the mail. I'll soon have millions again.

Do you suppose we could learn to eat these things?

The other thing I noticed in the cleaning ordeal is that order is brittle.

What I mean is this. When my wife and I stored all this stuff away long ago, including the peanuts, we did so neatly. We put big, heavy things on the bottom and small, light things on top. Everything was clean and in good condition.

But when we began our cleaning, we discovered a shambles. Stuff was filthy, broken, and disordered.

How did this happen? Have we had occasion to dig a few things out in the last year or so? Has dust settled from the air? Have cardboard boxes weakened? Have loads shifted, stacks of stuff collapsed?

Maybe so. Anyway, we did our re-packing with an awful feeling that we were just creating the illusion of good order.

No matter how orderly it is now, in two weeks it will be a dump, and neither of us will want to touch it, and we won't touch it until we run out of room and have to.

Those are my two discoveries: mostly we have peanuts, and order is brittle. Life is more transitory, less elegant than I wish it were. The work of a lifetime degenerates sooner or later to artificial peanuts and disorder.

No ma'am: you don't protect the order you create by packing it with peanuts. We just have to keep cleaning up and throwing stuff away. Next to godliness, they say.

THINGS PEOPLE DO

Follow Your Dream to Whitney, NE

One Saturday a few years ago I was sitting down for lunch when I had a mysterious revelation.

"There ought to be a town named Whitney, Nebraska; and if there is, I should retire and move there!"

I mentioned this revelation to my wife, and proposed that I ought to go right away to the computer and check it out. Is there such a place? Is it our destiny?

My earth-dwelling wife, however, pointed out that if a Whitney, Nebraska, existed, it would still exist when I had finished lunch. Lunch was, as I recall, a grilled cheese sandwich and tomato soup, and she probably used words like "gluey" and "cold."

I ate in a frenzy, and retired immediately to the computer in search of Whitney, Nebraska.

And lo! such a place exists!

It's a small city, to be sure: population "approximately 38." I don't know what margin of error is responsible for the "approximately" part, but it's clearly subtle.

And Whitney is not located near any major population centers. Its nearest significant neighbors appear to be Laramie, Wyoming, and the moon.

Still. I felt I had been given a momentous directive. "Rise up and go to Whitney!"

I proposed to my wife that we travel there to see what it is like. The software worked out a route, and I was a little dismayed to find that we would just about have to drive, since there's no airport anywhere near Whitney. The days-long drive would take us across the usual interstate highways, but then trickle down to lesser and lesser roads until we had to catch the right turn on Nebraska State Route 20 N.

I had visions. Cheap real estate—a vast holding in beige-colored mountains for a few bucks? Clear, pure water? Cheerful, welcoming people who play chess well? Peaceful valleys, glowing sunsets, millions of crystal stars at night?

My wife seemed less interested than I. She grew up in south Texas, and has seen her share of small dusty towns.

I looked up Whitney on the Internet. No mention of shopping. No real estate listings available. No tourist attractions. No hotels. No college. No airport.

And, to be fair, I could see why, for only approximately 38 people.

So my vision gradually changed. My new expectation included an abandoned drive-in movie, a convenience store, a Dairy Queen, and maybe an American Legion hall. A few people who commuted to Laramie to work every day, and spent evenings huddled over stamp collections or stunned by TV.

My problem, you see, is that like everyone else, I was brought up believing that we should, at all hazards, follow our dreams. If a destiny appeared mysteriously in one's mind, then it was probably glorious.

But I began to think maybe there are dreams and there are dreams. Maybe this vision came to me by way of thought waves sent by gangsters, whose M. O. was to lure me to Whitney, Nebraska, there to beat me, strip me, rob me, and leave me beside SR 20 N.

I had to consider that possibility.

And eventually I determined, with the help of my wife, to use this revelation concerning Whitney in a different way. It will fulfill the romantic concept of the road not taken, the vision of Xanadu that vanishes when a man from Porlock knocks at the door.

Yes, that's it. I'll use Whitney by never going there. Someday I'll look winsomely at the aforementioned wife and say something like: "No matter what happens, my dear, we'll never have Whitney, Nebraska."

Makes your heart go all soft, doesn't it?

The Great Yard Sale Adventure

We had everything in the garage, most of it price-tagged and ready.

Here's the plan: my son and I would go before breakfast and post signs around. Meanwhile my orderly wife would eat a bit and finish price-tagging the merchandise.

When Ben and I got back, we'd catch a bite and start hauling stuff out onto the driveway for our big sale.

We had decided on an undersell strategy: just simple signs saying YARD SALE and our address, with an arrow.

We put one at the head of our little cul-de-sac, and then drove off to nearby street corners to post the rest. We figured six or eight would do nicely.

But as we returned, we noticed a cars swarming in our street. We began to take alarm.

We got home to discover our lawn and garage buzzing with strangers.

My wife had gone from "orderly" nearly to "frenzied."

She grabbed my arm. "They were all over the garage," she said as she had once said when speaking of some ants. "They broke in somehow. They're everywhere! They've started giving me money!"

No breakfast, then. My wife took money and made change—and apprehended would-be thieves—while Ben and I lugged the remaining goods out to the driveway, furiously price-tagging whatever we could.

Our lawn and driveway were clogged with strangers, wanting to buy everything. One fellow made me an offer on our mailbox.

"You've got this here priced too low," they told us. "So don't buy it," I answered. (But then I raised the price.)

We tried to close the garage door so people wouldn't take everything we owned, but feared killing customers. So we left it open.

One lady, rummaging in the garage, came across a clear plastic drop-cloth, spattered, torn, and grimy. It was in a corner with the sort of sweep-up that gets into garages: scraps of paper, old leaves, dead spiders.

"How much you want for this here?" she asked.

"Lady, that's trash," I said. "Not for sale."

"How much?"

"OK, then, fifty cents, then."

She pointed to my son. "That guy over there said I could have it for a quarter."

One guy bought a heavy pocketful of old nails, screws, washers, and orphaned keys for a dollar.

People roared up to the curb in low-slung booming cars, strode around announcing how bad the merchandise was, and buying fifteen or twenty dollars worth of stuff well worth discarding.

Late in the afternoon, when we had exchanged most of our energy and detritus for hard cash, a family drove up: sad looking man and woman, several pasty looking kids.

"I heard you had some kids furniture."

"Yes," I said, imitating a sales clerk. "Inside. Come on in."

I showed them a bunk bed set, plain and sturdy. Probably the best thing in the sale, a bargain at $40.

"Well, that's nice. But we ain't got no $40. My husband he's laid off with a bad back and I got the dyebeedus and can't work neither. We really need that bad, the younger kids got no place to sleep except on the floor or in a chair or something. But we ain't got no $40. They just going to have to do without, I guess."

Well, you can see where this is going. I sold them the beds for $20, and then my son and I had to haul them out and tie them to the car, owing to the husband's bad back.

As they got into the car, the husband told his wife, "Well, that's the same as what we spent yersdiddy for that lawn furniture."

The Red Dodge of Carriage

It has always seemed to me that a pickup truck should be red. A worn, dusty shade of red that takes a few years to develop.

I'm not completely sure why I think that. Perhaps it's because where I grew up, that's the kind of pickup people used when they had some work to do. And then, when the workday was over, they went on dates in it.

It was common on Saturday night to see a dull red pickup truck pulling into the drive-in movie with a fellow of about seventeen at the wheel, and snug beside him, in the middle of the seat, a girl around the same age, with a ponytail. Often as not, she was turned completely sideways, looking at the side of the boy's face. The license plate might be bent or muddy.

My friend Jimmy had such a truck, and I tried to buy it from him after we graduated from high school. I thought it would be perfect to move my stuff to college with. But Jimmy demurred, saying that I didn't want to look like a hayseed among the smart college men and women. A lot he knew.

The first Datsun pickup I ever met was the first white pickup I ever saw. I thought it looked kind of antiseptic, like a truck you would haul supplies to a clinic with. I was uncomfortable around it. It seemed too clean.

Black is OK for a truck, but I don't know about green. I think they use green pickup trucks in California, if you take my sense.

But the issue is not the base color. The problem is that if you buy a new pickup truck, the paint will be bright and shiny. This looks like the kind of truck that advertisers want us to believe yuppies take their wives or dates to nightspots in.

It is a ridiculous fantasy, but that is what they want us to believe.

No self-respecting person can drive such a truck. To drive this truck would be to associate oneself with the kind of person for whom a truck is a stylish affectation. The kind of person who would buy several hundred dollars worth of plywood just so he would have something to haul around.

This kind of person drives a pickup truck to pretend he is not actually this kind of person. Of course, the affectation betrays the pretense, but such people are not famous for self-awareness.

Where do you get such a truck, one with a little age, a little character to it? One that has known honest toil? A populist truck, so to speak.

Don't tell me you buy it used. I am not that dumb. When a person owns a good, useful truck, he or she does not sell the truck just to be selling it. He sticks with it until the bitter end. The truck must be hopelessly beyond use to be up for sale.

Any truck you can buy used is one you should not. Any truck you should buy, you cannot. It's a tough problem.

I have decided that you cannot buy these trucks. To be sure, the starter kits for them are for sale: you get the basic chassis and engine and wheels and the like. It's called a new truck. But the color is all garish and wrong. You buy it anyhow, if you need it, and you work with it for a few years.

Gradually it becomes a truck you can be proud of. You can't buy such a truck, really. You have to earn it.

A Confession Involving The Saxophone

I have to confess to a prejudice. I'm afraid I just don't have a good attitude about the saxophone.

This is not about the people who play saxophone. Well, not all of them. It's the instrument itself. Or rather, itselves. Is there such a word?

You see, saxophones, like currency, come in many different denominations. The smallest is the soprano saxophone, which is about the size and shape of a smallish baseball bat.

Like some major league baseball bats, the soprano saxophone is hollow. Unlike those bats, it is not stuffed with cork. Alas.

For the sound of the soprano saxophone is shrill and piercing, like certain electronic devices manufactured by Honeywell. For me, an evening with a soprano saxophone is a bit like being stabbed in the ear with something rusty.

Then there are the familiar alto and tenor saxophones, which play in more reasonable ranges and are, I'll admit, much easier on the ear. But their sound is, to my ear, essentially uninteresting. It is the Cheez Whiz of instrumental sounds.

To compare, consider the sound of a well-played oboe. This is a mixture of anise, starlight, and elegant mathematical proof. Or the sound of a clarinet, which is like being happily alone in the forest, with a conscience as clear as a kitten's.

The alto and tenor saxophones, by comparison, are yesterday's newspaper. They are the magazines on the dentist's coffee table.

They are like attending a long meeting in one of those plastic chairs that you keep sliding out of.

There is also a baritone saxophone, a huge galoomphing thing that is best played by older males. Long ago, well before I was eligible, I tried to play baritone saxophone.

This was in a high-school "dance band." We played favorites like "Somebody Bad Stole de Weddin' Bell." and "Papa Loves Mambo." My task, concealed behind the great brass coils of this immense engine, was to get it to make big "bahh-DOOP!" sounds at appointed times.

I had a mouthpiece the size of a moon pie with a reed whittled from the cover of a three-ring binder. I affected a raffish posture, but produced few convincing bahh-DOOPs.

I think there may at one time have been a bass saxophone, but you won't see many of those. Word is that the Russian Navy bought them all up to refit them as a submarine fleet.

Actually, I find saxophones, with their callow, offhand sound, just fine for light, recreational music. Remember Les Brown and the band of renown? Good saxophone players there.

But unfortunately, when people try to play serious music on saxophone, the incongruity of it subjects them to behavior disorders. They fall to posturing and mugging, rather than just playing the music.

There are two postures universally affected by solo saxophonists. Both require the eyes to be squinted inexorably shut.

In one of these, the soloist holds his or feet close together, and leans dangerously backward, raising the instrument (and the performer's nostrils) into the air. The face takes on a look of wild emotion, either anguish or ecstasy. You can't tell, and I don't think it matters, because it is the same expression for all music, all performers, all venues.

The other standard posture is with one foot forward, the body bent over at the waist, elbows out. Here the performer affects a scowl of glowing intensity. Once again, irrespective of what is being played, or by whom, or to whom.

I'm aware, now, that I am wrong, dead wrong, in this bias. What can I say? I'm a flawed guy.

But at least I know.

A Mountaintop Experience on a Rooftop

I was thinking recently about a genteel little joke my grandmother used to tell.

Seems there was a minister who was horrified and offended by the new fashion in ladies' hair styles—the topknot. Obviously this was a few years ago.

This minister's outrage reached its height when his wife came home one day with a topknot. He instructed her peremptorily to take it down.

But she demurred, and said there was no reason for him to object to her hairdo.

Indeed there was, he insisted. It is immoral!

Well, I'll spare you the obvious developments, but the upshot is that they made a deal. If he could find scriptural authority for his position against the topknot, she would comply. If he couldn't, she wouldn't.

Next Sunday, after unusually long and determined labor in his study, the grimly satisfied parson climbed into the pulpit and triumphantly announced his text for the day:

"Let him who is on the housetop not come down!"

History does not record whether this worked, but there's my grandmother's joke for you.

The trouble with me is that I can't help thinking of the wrong thing at the wrong time.

I was musing on this joke the other day as I hunched along my roof trying to unclog some gutters.

Paul Cox

I had better things to be thinking of at that moment: the peril to my aging body. The unpleasantness of my task The impressions the gritty shingles were making on some very impressionable parts of me.

How effectively the gutter guards I installed had trapped stuff in the gutters.

And mostly I should have been thinking how stupid I was to forget how unbelievably hot a roof gets on a sunny morning. I had clambered up in shorts and was now paying the price.

My helpful wife offered to serve roasted jackass for dinner. I thanked her appropriately.

No, she didn't really. I can't have you thinking she's all that cruel, or all that witty.

Actually, she was a big help: she held the ladder. Except when her attention wandered.

I'm not exactly afraid of heights, you understand. But I get kind of edgy when I am conspicuously high up and there isn't anything very secure underneath me.

This may seem to others like craven cowardice, but it seems to me a natural and healthful caution. I come from a long line of earth-dwellers.

Anyway, I mucked around in the gutters until all the trapped water trickled thankfully down its assigned spout. I cleaned away millions of those ragged yellow floppy things from trees that deliver pollen to my lungs.

It can get tricky to sneeze satisfactorily on a rooftop without throwing your back out. Take it from me.

All birds, cautious fellows themselves, made themselves scarce. Bees, on the other hand, genially offered their help, even after I waved them off.

Meanwhile neighbors, curious why colorful shouts should be resounding from the heavens, came out to spectate.

I could picture other neighbors, terrified, calling TV news departments and the sheriff's office with dreadful news: "You better come quick! It must be awful!"

Of course, eventually the moment I most dreaded arrived. I finished my work and had to come down.

If you share my little acrophobic vulnerability, you know that the hardest part of any such exercise is climbing down. Staying up there seemed like a good alternative.

I considered just tumbling off the roof in preference to the terror of trying to locate an invisible ladder with my trembling toe.

That's when I thought the preacher in my grandmother's joke had a good point.

Beam Me Ever Upward, Scotty

My terrestrial wife keeps insisting I need a longer ladder. As you may know, I recently spent some time on top of my house. A friend remarked that this was bad for the roof. I appreciated his solicitude on behalf of the roof, and may cut him out of my will. Big threat.

I was up there for about an hour, and then spent an agonizing lifetime trying to get back down. The reason for this problem could be attributed to the ladder, which is, you see, rather brief.

It's a sturdy, squatty kind of aluminum stepladder, festooned with yellow warning tags describing the many ways a person can fall. The message of these tags is: this ladder is too dangerous for human use.

It reaches up to maybe eighteen inches below the edge of the roof at the roof's lowest point. Mounting the housetop thus involves traversing a foot and a half of nothingness. Coming down means blindly traversing this foot and a half with a foot and a toe—an act of incredible faith.

It's this encounter with nothingness—a major theme of the 20th century, of course—that makes the passage perilous, terrifying and, ultimately, magnificent.

There are several poetic ways to describe it.

"Effecting the synapse between earth and heaven."

"Bridging the cosmic divide with the human form."

"Completing emptiness with corporeality."

You will forgive me, I hope, if all this sounds a bit glorious. It just doesn't seem appropriate to use everyday, dirt-bound language to discuss such a breathtaking ascent.

Where's the thrill in saying "climbing up on the roof"?

When I ascend to the rooftop, do my work, and make it back down alive, I am renewed. There's nothing like it for growing one's inner self. For reaffirming courage. For overcoming limitation. Oh, yes.

My wife, however, has a different perspective. While I was up above looking down, she was standing with both feet on the earth looking up.

She thinks we need a longer ladder.

This is a recurring conversation. Her position in it is, it seems to her, relentlessly practical. Our present ladder is dangerously short. It does more to impede our altitude-oriented chores than to advance them, owing to the element of terror it introduces into the preparations. It makes us look ridiculous. She's tired of discussing it over and over. Therefore we need a longer ladder.

I believe my position trumps hers easily.

First, I am, it seems to me, as relentlessly practical as she is. The ladder limits us to mostly safe jobs. And we need a longer ladder too seldom to justify the cost.

Besides, say we bought a long ladder. To do us any good, it would have to be really long, and it wouldn't fit into the car. How are we going to get this wonderful long ladder home? And what good would ownership be without actual on-premises possession, huh? Huh? Well?

Second, my position has poetic merit.

With our present ladder I get to experience occasional confrontations with my soul. I get to frog-walk around on top of the house, head in the sky, thinking elevated thoughts.

And besides, if we got a longer ladder, then what would we have to talk about? Laundry, I think, and that's certainly no fun. I mean, after all, laundry?

We have an exalting subject in this ladder conversation, one with heaven-and-earth implications, and we should hang onto it, for goodness' sake.

A man's reach, you see, should ever exceed his grasp. Else what's a heaven for?

I'm pretty sure Elizabeth Barrett Browning never nagged her husband about his ladder.

Home Maintenance Made Easy

Minor repairs around the house are simple if you have invested in the correct tools and know how to use them.

Let's start today's lesson with an easy task. A thingy that holds a roll of paper towels has pulled off the kitchen wall, leaving a smallish peephole in the drywall. Your job is to get the towel holder back up.

You will need the following tools: a screwdriver. A screw. A thing that anchors the screw in the drywall.

These are in the basement near the water heater. Go.

In the basement are also some cartons of old *Life* magazines that your great aunt left you. There's a picture of Marilyn Monroe when she was young. With Joe DiMaggio—what a ball player! Oh, and remember that picture of President Truman holding up the copy of the *Chicago Tribune*—"Dewey Wins!"? Gee.

This part of the task may take awhile, but eventually you remember what you came for and liberate your yellow toolbox from the basement spiders. Go back upstairs. Come back for the screwdriver. No lollygagging with the magazines.

You have several different shapes of doo-jiggers to anchor the screw into the drywall. Most of them don't work, but you can't remember which. Some look like little blue or red cigars, others like bullets, others like surgical devices.

So you pick one that seems about the right size. It should fit snugly.

But, of course, it doesn't: too tight. The hammer's in the basement, so you must tap the anchor into place gently with a small pan.

This test proves what you feared: that the drywall isn't sturdy. Now you have a much more commodious hole in the wall, one you could occupy with a saucer.

You now have two options. One is to plug this hole somehow. The other is to buy a new towel rack that's larger than the hole. This you will simply attach over the hole with Krazy Glue. Should work.

You head for the hardware store. There you meet Ed, whose book is due to be published any day now, and discuss it with him.

Also you get really interested in the devices that people have invented for dealing with mailboxes: cute gadgets that show whether you have mail; clever contrivances to attach your name and street address to the mailbox; cunning doohickeys to anchor the box into the earth without much work.

Smart, these mailbox people.

Eventually you remember why you came, and locate a new towel holder. The only one that seems big enough, though, also hangs various little hand-appliances, and costs $49.95. But what can you do? Besides, this is a really clever fixture, and may effectively double as a Valentine's Day gift. Hey!

A smart shopper, you remember to buy Krazy Glue. Also some epoxy in two little colorful tubes: you may need this for something someday, and besides, it's really neat.

Back home. You stick the towel holder to the wall with the Krazy Glue. Make certain it's perfectly level, and that it's high enough so the hand appliances don't drag on the counter. You're doing a great job. Hold it tightly in place while the glue sets hard. As you do, notice how it's upside down.

You yank your hand away in alarm, but it's glued to the fixture.

Now the hole in the wall is large enough to crawl through.

OK, good! You've done it! You no longer have a minor household repair to deal with!

It's a major problem now, and someone else can deal with it. Get on the phone and call a professional.

Helping Daddy Around the House

My Daddy is the smartest man in the world. He can fix anything, especially when I help.

Here's how Daddy and I fix a broken light switch.

A broken light switch is when the light doesn't come and you can't see. Mommy tells Daddy: "Honey, the light in the pantry is out."

Now, Daddy likes to fix things, so he throws down the paper and hollers, "Oh great! Just great! I'm going to have to fix that switch."

First we have to get our tools.

Daddy keeps his tools in the basement, and I keep mine in my room. I have a big yellow skdiber that I use to twist screws out with, a bammer that I pound with, and a nice hercha that I cut things with.

When I have my tools, I run to the basement to help Daddy. He is over at the spider box staring at little handles. He hollers to Mommy: "Honey, tell me when I get the right one." Then he moves one of the little handles, and the basement gets all dark. So Daddy hollers "Honey, bring me a flashlight."

After we holler a lot of times really loud, she comes with the flashlight. It doesn't work, though, because I squirted out all the light into Daddy's eyes when it was new. So Mommy gets the flashlight from the car instead. Daddy turns the handle back, and the light comes on.

Daddy turns several handles until he has the right one, and we go to fix the light switch, while Mommy watches football.

This is the funnest part.

Daddy puts his skdiber up to the wall and turns it. So do I. Then pretty soon a screw comes out of the wall, and Daddy asks me to hold it. Then another one comes out, and he wants me to hold that.

Holding the screws is very important, so I put them in a safe place.

Daddy pulls wires out of the wall. "All right, Jason," he says to me. "Tell me what's the problem here."

"The light doesn't come," I remind him.

Daddy twists the wires and pulls them apart, and puts them back together. I don't have any wires, so I pound on the wall with my bammer.

Pretty soon Daddy says, "Well, Jason, let's see if that did the trick." And I answer, "I think it did the trick." "You think so?" Daddy asks. "Yep, I think we did the trick," I say.

So we go back down to the spider box. Daddy holds me up and asks me to turn the handle real carefully. I do, and we hurry to the pantry, but the light didn't come.

"I don't know what's wrong with the stupid thing," Daddy tells Mommy. Of course, he really does, but he's playing a joke on Mommy.

"Did you try changing the bulb?" Mommy is still watching football.

"Did you try changing the bulb?" Daddy says to me in his squeaky voice. Then he hollers to Mommy: "It isn't the bulb!"

Daddy fixes some more, while I pound with my bammer and tell him jokes. But when football stops and the TV man yells about beer, Mommy brings Daddy a new light bulb that she has been hiding for a joke.

Daddy hollers, because he thinks Mommy's joke is funny, and screws in the new bulb, and the light comes.

"Good thing I got those wires tightened first," Daddy says. Mommy agrees: "Oh, yeah," so I say "Oh, yeah" too.

Then Daddy and I have more fun looking everywhere for the screws.

And that's how we fix things around the house and have fun on weekends.

Choosing a Barbershop

"No barber pole out front, you don't go in."

I had asked Peter, my barber in Chicago, whether he had any advice for me, moving to Brevard, NC. I had come to rely on Peter for advice in various areas of my life. His expertise embraced both head and heart. Maybe I should explain.

I had discovered Peter kind of by accident, when a fancy hair stylist shop I had been unhappily patronizing had stood me up. I had an appointment; they had somebody fancier to accommodate. Peter had a cancellation.

Peter is about my age, and it turned out, like me a fitness swimmer. This means neither of us was really a good swimmer, but we swam a few times a week because it was a way to stay in some kind of shape. He had had a heart bypass, and he likes Greek cooking (well, he is Greek, see). So we got along well. He advised me on cardiac fitness from a standpoint of experience.

"Listen to your body," he told me one day. "It will tell you what you need to do."

If you're curious, here are Peter's rules for selecting a barber in a new town. Women don't need to read this part.

First, go to a barber. Not a stylist. Not a beautician. Nothing against those, but cutting men's hair is different. Different conventions. Different skills required. Different training. All different. Go to a barber. Peter insists on this.

Second, go to a barber your own age. He (or she: nothing sexist in all this) will understand what you need. "What if I want to look like Brad Pitt?" I asked.

"You don't want to look like Brad Pitt. You want to be what Brad Pitt hopes he will grow up to be." I thought that made pretty good sense.

Third, look at the people in the shop. The customers. The other barbers. Are they funny-looking? If so, ask politely whether there is a hardware store nearby, and leave.

But here I differ a little from Peter. See, Peter really believes in cutting hair well. This matters to him in the way good basketball matters to Michael Jordan. But I have a little more tolerant standards. I went to a barber in Indiana for a few years, who was so inept his kids refused to let him cut their hair. But Richard was a great guy, and his shop was the site of the funniest conversations I ever listened in on. Guys had been coming to him for decades, going out looking terrible, and grinning from ear to ear. This is the kind of shop Peter never would have understood, but I liked it. Too bad about looking stupid, but it was a fun shop. An exception to the rule.

Once you choose a barbershop, here is what you do.

First, you can give the barber instructions the first few times you sit in the chair. You say: "I want it down to the tops of my ears on the sides, and just a little bit tapered in back. No neck shave." And that is pretty much it. You don't go into detail, and you don't get silly with it. You don't take more than a sentence or two. The barber nods and generally does what you want. And after a couple of times, once the barber has had time to get you in his (or her) head, you don't do that, either. It would be rude.

My wife doesn't understand this: she expects that the barber and I must surely have a long consultation, and that the conceptual side of the operation is something we work out in depth. Nope. I give him a general sort of outline, and trust he can handle the rest of it. This allows me to concentrate on conversations about TV shows, vacations, and high school football.

Second, you observe the waiting conventions. These are simple, but critical. First come, first served. If you want a particular barber, you indicate this by pointing at him and smiling briefly, saying his name: "Peter." This means you forfeit your place in the waiting line, but get the next shot at Peter. If the shop takes appointments, and you are on time, you don't wait. This is the barber's lookout: he is traffic cop. But whatever the barber decides, that is it. These are the rules. As a newcomer, you don't mess with the rules.

Third, you enter only gradually into the conversation. This varies from shop to shop, but generally turns on weather, family, and high-school football. It is wholesome, cheerful, and pleasant. It is spiritually nourishing, in an odd way. Makes you feel calm and good about life. But don't join in all at once. Listen for a time or two before you speak.

Anyway, I followed Peter's advice. I found a barbershop in Brevard that has a barber pole in front of it. The barbers there are a little younger than I am, but they are clearly serious about life, so this adds to their essential gravity. They understand how to cut a man's hair. The shop is pretty quiet, actually. I don't get the kind of free-flowing, off-beat, male sort of fun conversation I might prefer. But I get that at the chess club. Which is another subject.

How to Speak the Special, Horrific Language of TV

You may have noticed that TV people speak a different language from the rest of us. I freely admit that my having observed this phenomenon shows that I waste far too much time. I can't deny it.

But I'll try to redeem that wasted time with a scientific observation: TV people talk funny. It's true. Here are a few examples.

You may have noticed that in the last year or two TV has tumbled to the word "horrific." This appears to be an advanced way to say the same thing that we used to mean by "horrible." But, you see, "horrific" seems to be a blend of "horrible" and "terrific," so it has more pizzazz. Everything on TV that is bad is now "horrific." A "horrific" fire. A "horrific" wreck. A "horrific" crime.

Ordinary, non-TV people are now beginning to use this word, of course. Pretty soon we will weaken it down as we do most others, and will speak of having a "horrific" time at a bridal shower. Well, maybe that won't be completely off the mark.

Another interesting thing TV announcers do is stress prepositions. Typically this is for non-smiley news stories: "The alleged assailant fled FROM the scene." "The Senate votes ON the measure tomorrow." Notice that nobody in real life talks this way. We just slide the prepositions ("with," "of," "to," and so on) in where we need them and keep going. Not TV reporters: they like to sing the prepositions out like little anthems. "Here's Herkimer Spondee WITH the story!"

Of course, sports announcers are routinely kidded for their language. There is a long tradition in American sports journalism of using witty synonyms. That's still done, but the TV people now add excited interjections. Every home run elicits a cry of "BÖÖM" from the sportscaster; every long gain in football is narrated about an octave above normal range. This informs us, you see, that sports are exciting. OK.

Weather people don't have as much fun, but they want you to think they do. I mean, "boomer" is an adequate synonym for thunder, but, let's be honest: it's pretty boring, isn't it? The really witty, far-out weather people will go so far as to say "whoosh" and wave their arms to tell us about a weather movement. Yawn.

For the richest comedy, however, I prefer the regular news anchors. They always address one another by name, as if engaged in a conversation. The anchorperson asks the remote reporter, "Tell us, Herkimer: what was the scene like AT the accident site?" The remote reporter addresses both the anchors: "Well, Loomis and Artesia, it's pretty horrific."

Then the remote reporter jams a microphone in someone's face and says, "Tell us, Mr. Whatever, how did you feel when you saw your house, barn, car, and business go up in flames?"

Now, wouldn't you just once like to see Mr. Whatever give a completely straight answer, perhaps punctuated by a heartfelt chop to the reporter's throat? But they never do. "Felt pretty bad," is the usual reply. If he had been professionally trained, he would have said "horrific."

You may be expecting me to wind this up by saying I wish they would stop trying to talk fancy, and just say what they mean. But nosir, not me. I hope they find ever more loopy ways to bend the language. It's just about the only real good reason to watch.

The Mystery of TV Mystery

I'm always intrigued when TV detectives find a slip of paper in the vic's pocket. This usually happens when they don't know who the vic is.

Their problem: identify the vic, then try to find the perp. Got that? And there is no identification on the DOA (another snappy term for "vic") except this slip of paper—with seven digits on it. A phone number? Hey, good guess!

The detectives figure that it's something, at least. Might lead them somewhere. Of course it will: this is TV, after all. There is no such thing as a useless clue on TV.

So they head for the nearest phone and dial the number.

Ain't this fun? A whole new anonymous character is about to be introduced. And if you thought the vic was a mystery, just you wait and see who answers.

Ah, good. We start the hour with multiple mysteries, not to mention a capital felony, and we know that by the time the news crew gets to their desks for the 11:00 fires and crashes, all will be cleared up.

But as astute viewers, we aren't completely in the dark. We do know a few things about the case.

First, we know that if there is any character in the story who has a lot of money, as evidenced by a fancy car and a foreign accent—that's your perp.

Now, look out for this guy. He'll have an expensive, arrogant lawyer, and oily manners. But don't be fooled: you cannot be a wealthy person on a TV cop show without being also a felon.

This means, by the way, that if you have a taste for expensive clothes and cars, you must stay off TV. You will be arrested for killing somebody and convicted. This is a friendly warning.

Second, we know that the crime will involve either sex or illegal drugs or both. There is no option here: all TV crime boils down to these. The cops are always astonished, of course, but that is because being on TV, they never watch TV. They don't have our advantages.

Third, the detectives, even though they solve the most intractable, bewildering mysteries week after week, at enormous personal risk, with cleverness, energy, and heroism that the rest of us can only gape at—these detectives will be despised and distrusted by their department superiors.

Their bosses will always be threatening to fire them, or have them investigated or suspended.

Often the detectives do get suspended, but they keep right on working anyhow. Suspension just frees them from certain bureaucratic limitations. Dedicated mavericks, see—gotta love 'em.

Thus a well-trained audience undertakes the mystery of the anonymous vic with a phone number. Let's get to work.

The detectives dial the number, and what happens? Somebody answers! Can you believe it? Not a pizza parlor. Not a machine. Not a "menu of choices." An actual person—it's the miracle of TV, of course.

This person is invariably rude and evasive. In fact, all the people the detectives interview are rude and evasive.

Well, unless they are just garrulous nuisances. The detectives shrug these off with stoic resignation.

The detectives work through a bramble of lies, ambiguities, evasions, accents, expensive lawyers, bureaucratic obstacles, and of course, the distraction of person tragedies. And invariably at about 56 minutes past the hour, they collar the perp—the rich guy, now reduced to a sniveling heap—and he wails his confession.

Now somehow—we knew it all along. How did we get smart enough to solve these mysteries?

Well, we have pretty extensive training, don't we?

Your Preview of the New TV Season! (Also the Previous)

It's about time for the new season of TV shows, and like you, I'm all agog with excitement!

I don't know many specifics, but I'd like to review the new offerings for you, so you can begin now to plan your viewing schedules. You don't want to be caught unprepared, you know! Not when the excitement is in full swing!

First off, there will be programs featuring young, attractive women struggling to make it in the working world. These programs will fall into categories.

One category will present office workers. They don't ever actually work; instead they fuss with one another, discuss their romantic relationships, and complain. There will be smartly dressed pretty women and goofy, witless men who exchange insulting wisecracks among themselves and try to date the pretty women.

Strangely, even though the women also want to date the men, difficulties arise. Actors will alternate between looking frustrated but wise, and arranging romantic relationships with one another.

The second category features professional women. You can tell the difference because the professional women have curlier hair and wonderfully cute, precocious daughters with their own needs. They (the women, not their daughters) will be physicians, lawyers, judges, and social workers.

Actors will alternate between looking tired but wise, and arranging forbidden romantic relationships with one another.

There will be gritty police shows, where policemen and women mostly solve crimes involving one another. Actors will alternate between looking tough but wise, and arranging forbidden romantic relationships with each other.

There will be dramatic hospital shows, where the only people who are permitted to die are blood relatives of the hospital staff. Actors will alternate between looking sad but wise, and arranging forbidden romantic relationships with each other.

There will be reality programs, in which people in artificial situations play contrived games for fabulous prizes. Quiz shows where people like you and me answer or fail to answer pointless questions for fabulous prizes.

There will be situation comedies where daffy, adorable young people sit around and wisecrack about pretty much nothing for half an hour, while arranging romantic relationships with each other.

There will be hard-hitting news-magazine shows, where the real truth about public school finance in Kansas City is explored. Or trash-hauling scandals in Santiago, Chile. Or mustard inspection mischief in Liverpool. You get the idea.

Barbara Walters will say: "Remember: we're in touch, so you be in touch." What do you suppose that means? Does anyone care?

On weekends we'll see old movies with the good parts edited out "for television," and news analysis shows where people in suits yell insults at one another about issues, and then grin like old buddies.

There will, of course, be sports.

You can expect televised football several nights a week, and all weekend. This will comprise high school football, college, professional, and specialty football.

This last category includes women's football, football played on roller skates, football played by people carrying pails of water, and so on. As I said, details are skimpy: I am simply projecting from recent developments.

Spiffy commentators will divine what players and coaches are thinking, and prophesy what is about to happen. They will be wrong, and will exchange flowery compliments on their work and receive fabulous, well-publicized salaries.

There will also be baseball. Basketball. Car racing. Hockey. Soccer. Rodeo. Monster truck rallies. Lacrosse. Curling. Marbles. Professional bingo. Hog-calling.

As you can see, the networks spare no pains to bring us top-quality entertainment that ennobles as it amuses. The best in the world, no doubt about it!

The season starts pretty soon. Re-runs begin a couple of weeks afterwards.

The End of the Action-Adventure Era (for Me)

I have given up on the type of movies they call "action-adventure."

Now, I know this may seem a bold and perhaps subversive decision. So I'll explain myself.

I went to these shows dutifully for years, eating my barrel of popcorn and growing increasingly dissatisfied. Then I saw a movie a few years back that settled it for me.

This was something called *Faceoff*, with John Travolta and Nicholas Cage. In it, some experimental surgeon or maybe taxidermist somehow managed to switch the identities of two people by simply cutting the face off one and sewing it onto the other. And vice-versa.

Some of the details are murky, but it seems as if in at least one instance, the patient was suffering from multiple gunshot wounds.

In an action-adventure movie, though, a few gunshot wounds are like an allergy to cats in real life. No big deal.

When they began this radical facelift, I got tickled. I was wondering where the lungs were going to come out, and may have begun to chuckle. But I composed myself when I became aware of hard looks from my neighbors.

After the surgery, the two actors resumed your standard transcontinental hunch-driven pistol battle. Each intermittently annoyed the other with gunshots, but this didn't slow them down much.

They shot scores of other actors, too, most of whom graciously expired on cue, blew up some buildings, wrecked some cars, trashed a boat or two, and generally behaved the way frisky, shot-up action-adventure heroes do in a day's work.

I was uncomfortable because it was so stupid. I didn't mind the explosions or stuff like that, although after awhile they became boring. But it was just so dumb. Why bother to write dialogue in a movie like this?

When I was a kid playing cowboys, if a player got shot he or she could just holler "I came back to life" or something equally lame, and rejoin the game. In an action-adventure movie they don't even try that hard.

The explosions and shooting are just for fun, I guess, because they don't do any real harm. So they're boring.

In fact, the most interesting thing in this movie was the way in which John Travolta could be made up to look exactly like Nicholas Cage, and even sound and move like him, and Nicholas Cage looked and acted exactly like Travolta. Amazing.

I decided not to see any more such movies. They were just too stupid, too insulting. But then our son, a hockey fan, got to be an extra in one featuring Jean Claude Van Damm. Something involving hockey.

In this movie the hero, having had his shots, breaks out of and back into a hockey stadium in Pittsburgh while dangling by a rope from a dirigible or something. He shoots the bad guys and saves the world, or at least Pittsburgh, from international villainy. Made no sense, and we never even spotted our son in the stands.

Action-adventure villains are an odd sort. They are the most evil people you can imagine. Fashion now is to make them foreign drug smugglers.

For a time they were white South African drug smugglers: that seemed safe. But now South Africa has changed. Then Arab drug smugglers were the universal victims, but we have begun to realize that Arabs are no more evil than anybody else.

So the movies are having to go back to motion picture superstars as (drug-smuggling) villains. This proves that the tried-and-true, familiar solution usually work best.

It's all variations on a formula: villains, heroes, explosions, shooting, fires. It works, I guess.

But not for me. I'll find something interesting instead.

Columnist Explains Other People's Snoring

You may be a little perplexed by snoring. Most people have two specific questions: why do people snore, and why don't people hear themselves snore?

Fortunately, I have the answers.

I read a speculation somewhere that people evolved snoring as a way of warning other animals off. When you sleep, see, you are vulnerable. A lion could stumble upon you by luck and protract your slumber indefinitely.

But if you wedge yourself into a fork in a tree and set up a commanding snore, then the lion thinks you must be fourteen feet tall and irritable. He will go looking for something smaller, something that sounds less scary.

I have a different explanation. I think that snoring is related to the invention of the guest bedroom. At first, of course, this room must have been called something different, like the "Chamber of Blessed Silence."

Our ancestors would have delicately refrained from talking much about this room. They wouldn't have wanted to embarrass the snorer, who doesn't do it on purpose, after all. And who usually doesn't even really believe he or she is snoring at all (but more on that later).

So the extra bedroom must at first have been a little novelty, its purpose generally understood but gently left unstated.

There it sat, usually empty. What do you do with such a room? Why, you invite guests.

The guests arrive cheerfully, and everyone has a fine time. You grill something on the Weber, lounge on the deck, talk and enjoy. Somewhat later than usual, you announce bedtime, and retire to separate rooms.

Of course, then there's a problem. When all four of you snore, there is no spare bedroom, or Chamber of Blessed Silence, to escape to.

So when morning arrives, bringing with it the newspaper and the baseball scores, it finds four people trying to be civil despite not having slept much.

Next day: worse. And so on.

And now nature's grand strategy is fully revealed. Just as snoring has led to the development of the guest bedroom and the arrival of guests, so it leads next to an excellent reason for the guests to remember an appointment back home.

What they really have back home, of course, is their own Chamber of Blessed Silence.

Snoring, you see, bringeth guests and it taketh them away.

The other question is why people don't hear themselves snore. This one is easy.

It is better that nobody actually believe he or she snores. Snoring is loud, vulgar, and embarrassing. Of course, nobody does it on purpose, but those that do it sound appallingly crude.

Now, if we could hear ourselves making this unholy racket, we would be mortified. "I sound like THAT?" we could cry, and become dangerously depressed.

Nobody needs to know this kind of thing about himself or herself. We have our self-images to protect, after all. Our little idealized views of ourselves that are essential to our emotional health.

These images would never survive the experience of hearing our own snoring.

And they don't need to. The objectives of snoring don't rely on the snorer's awareness of what he or she is doing. So long as someone else hears it, snoring works just fine.

So there you have it: why we snore, and why we don't hear ourselves. Another mystery explained.

Note, by the way, that I take up this subject purely as a public service. I myself don't snore, but here's the oddest thing. My good wife has a recurring dream in which she hears someone snoring. She dreams this nearly every night.

Now that one is hard to explain.

An Issue of Social Dexterity

The winter holiday season imposes upon us demands of dexterity that clearly exceed human capabilities. Let me explain.

You go to a social gathering billed as "a few friends getting together to wish each other something or other."

You are issued the following gear: a cup of punch, several cookies, a napkin with a picture of a poinsettia on it, and a tiny plate. Your task is to eat the cookies delicately, drink the punch, mop yourself with the napkin, and wish a stranger something or other.

This is a demanding assignment, obviously, its difficulty compounded by two factors. First, you are in a room calibrated to hold the exact number of its occupants, so long as no one attempts to move or turn. Certainly not to elevate his or her elbows.

Second, your conversation is supposed to be audible over Garth Brooks (I guess) athletically singing pseudo-holiday music.

I was discussing this problem with a friend the other day over a cookie and a cup of punch and a napkin and a tiny plate. We agreed that it required skills we had never really developed.

I shared with him one strategy that I usually fall back on. It is to drain the cup of punch at the moment it is issued me. Just drink the whole thing down and get rid of the cup somehow, like in a planter or among the cushions of an overweight sofa. Then I will have a hand free, and that helps.

Another strategy that I didn't get to is this. I hold the cup between my left thumb and the adjacent finger. I slip the tiny plate between my little finger and ring finger on the same hand, kind of wedged against my palm to steady it.

For exercises like this, by the way, it is wise over Thanksgiving to develop a rounded paunch, which will serve you as an all-natural rest for one edge of the tiny plate.

The problem, of course, is the punch. You will spill this punch. You might just as well go ahead and pour it out on the rug right away, because that is where it is going to go anyway if you don't drink it immediately upon receipt. Believe me.

As we talked, my friend's wife said something that fetched me up short.

"Well, women can manage it. Too bad men have such trouble. I guess it's the extra chromosome or something."

What? Can this be true? Can it be that women have contrived a method for juggling the elements of this party meal, and not told us? Does this skill come to them so naturally that they just never thought to tell us? Or do they conspire to withhold it?

It must be true that someone on earth can manage this feat, and, come to think of it, it must be women. If only men populated the world, I don't think we would have parties with punch, cookies, poinsettia napkins and tiny plates. I can't feature it. The problem arose because for women it is not a problem.

I've concluded that we need better communication between the sexes. Men have already been told not to put empty punch cups behind the upholstery and not to spill punch on the carpet (because, I think, it stains).

Well, maybe it is time to tell us how to manage the cups, cookies, napkins and tiny plates in the first place. We could have fun, not spill stuff, and not feel the anxiety of ineptitude. Males could, in effect, join the party.

OK? In return, I'll cheerfully tell how to handle the noise problem.

Noises in the Night

Remember the city mouse and the country mouse? The city mouse couldn't get to sleep in the country because it was too quiet, and the country mouse couldn't get to sleep in the city because it was too noisy.

Well, don't you believe it. I've lived both places, and I'm here to tell you it isn't the amount of noise. It's what you're used to.

It's odd how people react to night noises. They seem bigger, closer, and more insistent than day noises.

The sudden CLUNK from the icemaker downstairs in the refrigerator sounds like a mountain falling on the house. This is followed by a busy, annoying WHIRR.

The rustle of a mouse in the wall sounds exactly like a team of robbers on their way up the stairs with weapons.

A car backfiring three blocks away sounds like a howitzer in your garage.

Everyone's pet peeve is a barking dog. There is no person alive today who doesn't have a story to tell about a dog barking at night. I know this to be true, because I've heard every one of those stories.

They seem to have one thing in common, and you know what it is, because you have heard the stories too.

Why does a barking dog bother us so much? Maybe because the sound of a dog barking is an ancient signal of warning for humans.

"What're you trying to tell us, Lassie?" Each BOW and WOW restates that our territory has been encroached upon.

You can't discuss this without getting around to the sound of snoring. When I was a kid, the sound of my father snoring down the hall was a comfort at night. I don't know why. The sound of my wife snoring nowadays seems somewhat less comforting.

Fortunately, I don't snore. Sure I don't.

When my agreeable wife and I lived in the middle of downtown Chicago, the first thing we noticed was the quiet. There was no traffic noise, no airplane noise, no people noise. It didn't hurt, of course, that we were 49 stories up.

There was one exception, however. Many nights around 2:00, a motorcycle rider roared through a long underpass about a quarter-mile from the house.

Such a sound from a camel would have got it expelled from the caravan on grounds of indelicacy.

The cops could never find out who was doing it. My candidate was Satan, but they didn't take me seriously. Otherwise it was completely quiet.

But now that I live out of town—and it's a fairly small town I live out of—I find that the night is alive with sounds.

Raccoons, opossums, and who knows what other nocturnal critters hold quadrilles on my deck. They disassemble my Weber and sometimes put it back together again.

Every breeze that blows makes the tired old trees sigh and creak.

Little tree toads, or whatever they are, celebrate all night with a persistent chant: CHEEKACHEEKACHEEKA, CHOOKACHOOKACHOOKA, and back and forth all night long.

I usually wind up picking sides and rooting either for the CHEEKA or the CHOOKA faction. I don't really care, you know: I just want them to get the issue resolved.

These are comforting sounds, though. If you listen carefully to them, concentrate on them, try to visualize who is out there making these sounds, you will fall quickly into a restful slumber.

And sometimes the outdoor sound is the little drum roll of a gentle spring rain, with the trickling counterpoint of water flowing down the downspouts in the corner.

That I find mighty easy to become used to.

Pray for the Lights to Go Out

The Golden Gate Quartet is a favorite gospel group of mine. The other day I was listening to a song of theirs called "Pray for the Lights to Go Out," while the weather turned nasty.

TV announcers told us, as they invariably do when the weather turns nasty, about people hoarding bread and milk. The people in the grocery store tell us it's true, too, as we gather our share.

My practical wife prepared for the recent bout of grisly weather by making a meatloaf and a big kettle of soup. The hearty red kind with chunks of meat and vegetables.

We made certain there was something to burn in the fireplace and that we had something interesting to read. What if the cable should go out, after all?

Of course, meetings and social engagements were cancelled. No newspapers, except for the *Transylvania Times,* which comes in the mail, despite sleet and gloom of night and other grisly-weather visitations.

We got ourselves good and ready, even knowing that the event is usually a little disappointing.

You fantasize about the house being packed in snow up to the gables, about being stuck indoors for days, drinking hot chocolate that you heated in the fireplace, reading books by lamplight, playing board games with the kids.

Tunneling through massive snow banks to the neighbor's house, where you can cluck together about the weather, confirm that each hopes everyone else is faring OK, and drink more hot chocolate.

Braving the weather to go sledding with the kids, and then hurrying inside red-faced and exhilarated to drink still more hot chocolate. It's a fun fantasy.

The reality falls short. There is some ice, enough to make your driveway slick. The snow matures to gravelly slush, which gets into your shoes within the first few seconds of your venturing out to get the mail.

The power generally stays on, or if it goes out, it's only out long enough to zap all the electronic clocks. Instead of reading by lamplight near the fireplace, you spend your time circulating through the house trying to figure out how to reset the clocks. Disappointing.

I guess we all retain a little residual cave-dwelling temperament. We like to be thrown back a few centuries to a time when home meant a roaring hearth, when food was heated over flames, when outdoors was out there and we were in here wearing wool on our feet and keeping unfashionably warm.

Where the family was all in sight, safe, warm, and dry. The kids not having to go to practice something, the parents not having to go to work or to meetings, the pets purring or tail-wagging, depending.

Now, in the Golden Gate Quartet's song, the event of the lights going out was a little different. It is a sly song about frisking up the atmosphere of a revival meeting with a little levity in unexpected dark. Fun, in a slightly different way.

And I suspect the basic point is nonetheless the same as what I have in mind.

It seems to me that we just periodically want to get yanked out of the regular world we have planned for ourselves and into a more primitive, older, darker world where we can let down our guard, be spontaneous, be isolated.

Where we can relax because the only other people around don't care what we look like. They know us already. Everyone is comfortable, secure, peaceful, and safe. At home in the deepest sense.

Isn't that true? Despite your expressions of dread and apprehension, don't you sometimes pray for the lights to go out?

About the Three (or So) Stooges

Here's some news for you: I am a male, and I think the Three Stooges are just dumb.

There. Now I feel much better. But not entirely at ease.

There is, you see, a myth abroad that worries me. The myth is that all normal, healthy American males think the Three Stooges (not to be confused with the Tenors) are riotously funny. That they are the very epitome of all that is risible, including the word "risible."

But I don't know that it's true. Let me tell you about a Saturday morning phenomenon I noticed as a child.

I went, as was my duty, to the movies with the other kids. As I recalled, this required thirty cents: fifteen for admission, ten for popcorn, five for a Coke.

The presentation always included either a cowboy movie or a jungle movie. Even both, occasionally. I didn't care for the jungle movies, by the way, and had to challenge myself to sit through them, no matter how scary the wild animal scenes got.

There was also sometimes an installment of a serial, and usually one or more short comedy features.

These were either what we called a "cartoon" (in color, drawn) or a "comedy" (black and white, live actors).

If the Three Stooges were to be on, everyone professed great delight. Oh boy, the Stooges.

But then during the Stooges part of the show everyone went to the lobby for the traditional box of popcorn and Coke. Including me.

As a service to you, I have pondered the meaning of this odd phenomenon. Why did the kids express such enthusiasm for the Stooges, and then walk out on them?

I think we got excited because we understood that was what was expected of us. We understood that normal, healthy American kids loved the Stooges (everyone told us so), and of course we considered ourselves to be NHAK (if I may so abbreviate it). Thus the enthusiasm.

But when the film actually got underway, we found it silly and boring. Thus the popcorn.

This failure of the hype to fit the reality didn't bother us in particular. We didn't think about it. Next time the Stooges were on, we said again, "Oh, boy! The Stooges!"

What impresses me is that the hype continues. TV and even newspaper columns (which I should assume would be above this kind of thing) routinely take it for granted that all males are overgrown kids who giggle helplessly at The Stooges.

So my distaste for them makes me a little apprehensive. Am I, um, not right somehow? Is there a missing gene? Have I wandered out of line at some point, dropped a beat and got out of step?

I don't really think so.

What I think instead is that it is pretty normal for us to live in a world where the hype and the reality don't fit. Where we are told day in and day out what we like, what we want, who we are—and then we find out different.

I'm sure you've had the experience of someone's telling you he or she has found something unexpectedly enjoyable.

With me, it's opera: people say they thought they hated opera until they actually attended one. I guess they think they need to confess that to me, but I don't know why.

The important thing, I think, is to be aware of what is hype and what is real.

Might as well enjoy life on your own terms, rather then letting the hype decide for you.

You could be stuck with the Stooges for your whole life.

What Did I Do When I Did It?

Once my daughter asked me what I did.
Well, I said, I'm a consultant.
"Sure," she said. "That's what you are, but I asked what you do. What do you actually do when you're being a consultant?"
There she had me.
So I decided I would try to tote up just what I actually did at my job. I made some appalling discoveries.
I talked on the phone. I wrote on a word processor. I read memos and maybe scribbled on them. Handled emergencies.
I sat around baffled some of the time—and that was part of my job.
I talked with colleagues. What about?
Well, clients' problems, to be sure, and how to help solve them. But also other things: baseball. Movies. Books. Vacations and kids.
Sometimes I visited with clients, and we talked. Maybe I spent a day or two telling them how to use some software. Whatever the circumstances, about all we did was talk. Maybe we just sat at a table and talked.
We called that "having a meeting."
I had a game I used to enjoy playing at those odd meetings with strangers. I made a point not to ask anybody's name before or during the meeting, and then my objective was to address everyone in the meeting by name before it was over, and to refer to some non-work thing in each person's life. Children, hobbies, and such.

Nobody but me knew I was playing this game, to be sure, but it was part of what I did. It gave me something to think about during meetings.

Anyway, my activity inventory seemed a little paltry. I found it hard to put my finger on just what I did that was worth getting paid for.

So I decided I would begin making TO DO lists for every day. I would take a few minutes at the beginning of each morning, draw up a list of the things I needed to do that day, and check off as I went along.

Then, I noticed, immediately after making the list I invariably put it down and did something that wasn't on it.

I thought: this is nuts. There's what I claim to do, but don't, and what I claim to intend to do, but don't. Why don't I make a TO DO list that states what I actually intend to do, and then do exactly that? Wouldn't that make sense?

I started making TO DO lists that actually reflected the reality of my day: Call my wife to find out what's for dinner. Tell Jerry the joke I heard last night. Contact some client and explain how to solve her problem. Try to figure out another client's dilemma. Go to lunch with Mark.

Then I looked over this list and asked myself: which of these things would anybody be willing to pay me to do?

Probably not the joke, or finding out what's for dinner. Explaining something to a client, OK. Looking out the window and pondering a problem—and also the traffic down below and what I was going to have for lunch—I didn't know. Still don't.

Curiously, I have old résumés from those days. If you were to read one of them, you would conclude: this guy must have been a real ball of fire.

Of course, that is what they were designed to make you think. But oddly, everything in them was true. I always accomplished things and left work tired.

But just when did I do what I was doing when I did what I did? That's what I want to know.

WHACK! It's a Blow to the Head!

I got home one day several years ago to find my son nursing a very sore hand. He didn't want to talk about it much, but his mother explained that he had tried his skill at martial arts. He decided to kroddy the garage, but the garage turned out to be a most worthy opponent.

Maybe he got this martial arts stuff from TV. Just as likely he got it from playground friends who got it from TV.

As far as I know there's nothing really wrong with martial arts. I never got into any of that sort of thing, but I've had friends who were pretty serious about karate (they didn't call it "kroddy"), and they seemed to get a lot out of it. Good exercise, good discipline.

But it seems as if TV turns everything into a cartoon. A parody, if you will. Martial arts on TV—and in movies—involves violations of all the known laws of physics, biomechanics, and common sense. People fly through the air spinning like pinwheels, precisely kicking whole teams of bad guys (who just happen to be standing around looking stupid). Then those bad guys crumple and another platoon rushes up to get kicked. When somebody gets punched, even if the punchist is a thin beautiful woman with expensive hair, there is a crack louder than a hand grenade. I find some of this hard to believe.

I think some people, perhaps like susceptible 4-year-olds, think maybe there really are people somewhere who do that stuff. They figure it's worth a try. If they're lucky, the only harm done is that they lose a round to the garage.

It's not just martial arts. Have you seen TV wrestling? It is a particularly stupid parody of one of my favorite sports. If you've ever watched real wrestling, high school, college, or AAU, then you know that wrestling is a great sport. It takes strength, quickness, smarts, and psychological toughness. Not much luck, not much equipment, just two wrestlers out on a mat.

Once there was an NCAA champion, a 198-pounder, as I recall (this was a long time ago). He had the misfortune to graduate without any marketable skills except wrestling, so he turned pro. There he was on TV trying to pretend to wrestle: slapping the mat, letting opponents get miraculous escapes, yelling and boasting. He was very bad at it, and didn't last long. The pity was, he outlasted his dignity.

And I recently saw part of a show called something like American Gladiators, where sculpted men and women in gaudy outfits played contrived and rather silly games against one another. I don't know why they do that, really, because I didn't finish the show. But it seemed like yet another parody of legitimate sports.

I could go on and on. TV shows seem to parody everything they touch. Even angels, theologically respectable if not universally accepted, get parodied in a grossly sappy TV show. (Fortunately I have this little button marked ON/OFF that I can use.)

But you get my point: TV likes to take our perfectly enjoyable world and regularly convert it to nonsense. We have not heroes but phony superheroes. Not criminals but master criminals. Not real games but outlandish "extreme" sports. On and on: the normal world isn't exciting enough. It has to go beyond the normal world.

Of course, the ancient Greeks did the same thing, and I guess they turned out all right. But still, it seems to me an odd way to bring up kids. Ka-POW! A savage chop to the common sense.

Selecting a New Car

My wife and I thought it was time to buy a new car, so we went to a large dealership. We looked at a Sports Utility Vehicle, or APC.

"Oh, no sir," the salesperson said. "This is called an 'SUV.' 'APC' stands for Armored Personnel Carrier, a big, armored vehicle that carries lots of soldiers."

"Right," I said.

We were looking at a car that would seat nine adults. We tried to figure out who they would be. My wife and I, of course, and our daughter and son and their spouses. That's six. Then we figured Michael Jordan, the soprano Mirella Freni, and of course, Christina Applegate. That's the full nine, and we wouldn't have anyplace to put Senator Edwards, if he should need a ride.

We asked the salesperson: "If we have nine people in this car, can we also carry a rug in it?"

"Depends on the rug, sir," he said, nodding.

"I thought so," my wife said knowingly. "That's what they always say."

When we test drove this car, we discovered that we were seated up rather high. We could see down to the road, and could make out other cars, but they didn't seem to matter much. We were tempted just to drive right on over or through them if one should be in our path. So we decided to look at something smaller.

We asked about a compact car, but discovered that compact cars nowadays are quite a bit larger than we remembered last time we bought one. It used to be that a compact car was about like a lawnmower with doors. You putted along, close to the ground, and hoped that dogs stayed away.

Compacts now are bigger, more like what we thought of as luxury vehicles. What we had in mind was a sub-compact, like a gasoline-powered roller skate. But these, I think, are not intended for actual sale. I was thoroughly frightened when I was in one, and never did get up the courage to turn it on and try to drive it.

My wife thought we should consider just getting a large riding lawnmower and installing a heater in it. But we rejected that idea: too expensive.

Then we thought about a pickup truck. This might not accommodate nine passengers in full comfort, but if passengers were willing to sacrifice a bit, we could probably get even more than nine in it. If we disposed those passengers wisely, we could probably get a rug in it, too.

But we weren't prepared for the decisions we had to make. Four-wheel drive or two-wheel? (Three-wheel drive is not available.) Two, three, four doors? Plastic bed liner? Four speed? Five? Stick shift or automatic? Overdrive? Tape deck? CD player? Luxury interior? Air? Deluxe cup holders or regular? Bewildered, we gave up.

Not long ago a pickup truck was just a utility vehicle, and the options were: (1) take it or (2) leave it. But then the manufacturers made the error of showing commercials where yuppies went to dances and nightspots in them. Now pickup trucks must make a living during the week, and a fashion statement on the weekends.

Does that sound familiar?

Anyway, we dithered about the car awhile, and finally decided on a smallish compact with stick shift. It zooms down the road pretty well, doesn't use much gas, has a radio and a heater, and is painted. We can't get Michael Jordan in it (too tall), but otherwise I think it will do all right. No rug, though.

If Senator Edwards needs a ride, we're ready.

A Portrait of the Artist as a Young Dud

In my first year in college I met a fellow named Samuel—definitely not Sam. We were in a freshman music theory class: I because the subject interests me, and Samuel because he was a voice major.

He was a thoroughly decent person, but solemn. I don't remember ever seeing him smile. I remember an unchanging facial expression of serene and profoundly vacant frog-like solemnity.

Samuel was a baritone. His voice was loud and firm, if a little forced. His voice was keener, though, than his ear. To put it simply, he had a stone ear. Not good for a musician.

I learned this when he was called on to sing a C major scale in our class. This not hard. The other members of the class just *do-re-mi*-ed through various scales easily.

Samuel rose, however, for his performance, and sang his scale gravely, with massive dignity and effect. As his voice rose, so did his excitement. He grew progressively louder and sharper, and finally intoned his final mighty "*DO!*-uh!" at least a couple of tones sharp.

He had got completely off key within eight notes, and was the only person within earshot who didn't know it. Maybe the only person in the county.

Visibly moved, Samuel glared heroically around the room and resumed his seat. Nice fellow, you see, but never quite in tune.

Next spring I shared another class with Samuel—compulsory freshman P. E. A couple of early mornings each week twenty or so grumpy freshmen in purple shorts and numbered tee shirts gathered on a sloping field to play a compulsory game.

One morning a transformed Samuel came out in his purple shorts. I don't know whether this was his doing or whether mischievous roommates had worked with him, but he had determined to take up the manly practice of cussing.

But Samuel cussed the way he sang. He just couldn't hear it quite right. He was like a foreigner with an English dictionary: plenty of words, but no concept of idiom.

So he cussed everything he saw—with exclamation marks. He cussed every action he or anyone else took. He used nouns as verbs, threw adjectives about with no purpose, and generally garbled every sentence with pointless but potent cusswords.

A regard for decorum prevents my providing a verbatim transcript of his conversation on that morning, but here's how you can get the flavor.

Count to ten out loud. But before various numbers, throw in a cuss word or two—nouns, verbs, phrases randomly, the strongest you can think of. Do this emphatically and solemnly—just clutter the count with whatever rough scraps of the vilest vocabulary you can sweep up. That was how Samuel sounded.

The rest of us were convulsed with laughter all morning.

Samuel, meanwhile, gravely continued to brandish his new vocabulary with all the energy and vigor he had put into singing his scale—and with about the same effect.

Some people, you know, can throw a dash of lexical spice into a bland sentence at just the right point, in just the right tone of voice, and you have to admire. You might not approve, but you have to admire the skill.

Cussing is an art—not a fine art, to be sure, but something that can be done well by a skillful practitioner.

And Samuel, bless his heart, had no idea.

Well, unfortunately, Samuel completed his university experience in that one year. He really was a nice guy, and I sincerely hope he has gone on to a happy and rewarding life.

But not, I think, in the arts.

Living By the Rules

Do you know the rules? All the rules?

For instance, when are you justified in taking someone's clothes out of the dryer in a Laundromat? Under what circumstances are you justified in joining a line anywhere but the end?

(For instance, if your wife is in line, do you join her, or go the end of the line instead? Does she move back with you, or do you converse by shouting past the other waiting people?)

Which fork do you use for which course? The general rule is to work from the outside toward the plate as you work through the meal, but do you know all the exceptions?

Does the bride's biological father or stepfather give her away? Who dances with the bride's mother while everyone else watches, pretending to be choked up with emotion, but secretly criticizing his dancing?

Of course, specialty columnists make a comfortable living deciding on the rules to cover many of these circumstances. But there are others their wisdom doesn't reach.

What's the correct way, for instance, to tell the mechanic what you think is really wrong with the car, and how to fix it?

What should you do when you and another shopper reach simultaneously for the last one on the supermarket shelf? Is this a case where "he who hesitates is lost"? Or should you try to outwit the other person into taking the article, and at the cost of his or her dignity?

We need rules to cover these situations, or everyone loses. You either don't get the loaf of bread, or you get it and feel bad about it.

I know a person who always assumes that there is a rule, and that the rule means she can't do what she wants to do. "I think you're supposed to . . . ." is her favorite expression, and what you are supposed to do is whatever you would prefer not to.

This is where two classes of creatures have it all over the rest of us.

The first of these classes is all non-human animals. They have only a few rules, which don't require much explication. If you are bigger, you get what you want. Or quicker, or smarter, or meaner.

Unless you are a crow, in which case you are all of those, but you just prefer to squawk because squawking is fun.

The other class of people for whom rules don't count much is hockey goaltenders.

I don't watch much hockey, but I have noticed that these fellows have exactly one objective: to keep the puck from going past them.

If this means jumping for the puck in a way that breaks the legs of half your teammates, you jump for the puck.

If this means thrashing and flailing around on the ice like an idiot in front of a national TV audience, you thrash and flail with abandon.

Now, I would like to think that such a liberation from conventions and rules would mean that forest animals and hockey goalies were generally healthy and psychologically robust. But I don't know that they are.

Most of the goalies I know of consider themselves to be martyrs in some way: they put in more time on the ice, and get blamed whenever something goes wrong.

And most critters in the woods spend a good bit of their energy calibrating whether they are the intimidator or the intimidated—so they won't have to use rules instead.

Perhaps our submission to rules has some value for us after all.

And after all, the crows will probably get the last squawk anyway.

LIVING DANGEROUSLY

Living Dangerously - 1

Now there, I thought, is a man who is willing to live dangerously.

This was a father in the adjacent booth with two kids. The empty booster chair in the aisle testified to where the Mom was, and with whom. Dad was presiding when hotdogs and hamburgers arrived, and was presently applying ketchup to a naked hotdog.

The kids were questioning his order of operations, the pictures on the wall, the whereabouts of their brother and mother, why there should be so many sugar pouches. Which hotdog belonged to which kid? Why?

The dad patiently entertained as many of these questions as possible while vigorously saucing the dog.

His method caught my eye. It was a classic comedy-movie scene: a man banging the heel of his hand on the bottom of the ketchup bottle. The bottle was teasing him, dispensing dainty dabs, withholding the big red gush while the audience worked itself into a frenzy of suspense.

Here's the dramatic problem: Would Dad be able to stop one belt short of disaster? Or would he pound once too often and drench the weenie and himself in a ketchup cascade, making the children shout, and speckling his watch and shoes?

My mouth became dry with the suspense as he pounded, answered, pounded, administered napkins with whichever hand was loose, and pounded.

This is what I meant by living dangerously.

Somehow he got away with it. He pounded out just enough sauce to color the dog end to end, suddenly put the bottle down, passed the dish to his daughter and grabbed his burger. He had to hurry, see.

Because the wife came back with the youngest, the cranky one. Pretty soon the little diner table was a flurry of potato chips, napkins, little hotdog papers, soft drinks, conversation. Hands, teeth, fingers, glasses, sugar pouches were everywhere as the family set about their lunch.

At one point, without any hitch in his normal rhythm, Dad reached out and intercepted a hotdog just as the youngest was releasing it behind the booster chair toward the aisle floor. This was over before I fully registered what was happening: suddenly there was a loose hotdog and a hairy hand in the same spot where before nothing had been.

It was a miracle of anticipation and split-second timing. Astonishing to me, business as usual for him.

Pretty soon I understood why he was eating his burger so fast.

Little Cranky, who had tried to jettison the hotdog, became crankier. All parents know that the logical end of cranky is crying, followed by asleep. You've got to act fast.

There must have been a signal, because suddenly the father scrubbed his tiny napkin over his mouth, rose, picked up Cranky, and walked off to the gift section of the store, jiggling quietly.

The mother inherited the other two kids, and set about just as the father had done, deftly managing soda straws, questions, pickles and sugar pouches. Eventually the kids had had as much lunch as they wanted, so with a sudden swoop Mom gathered them up, and was off to join Dad and the Crank.

It was all so fast that the waitress wasn't entirely clear whether they had finished and left, or just vanished without a trace.

You want life on the edge? Take three small kids to lunch some day.

All this will pay off, you know, in twenty-five or thirty years. These kids, having seen how it is correctly done, will take their own energetic families to lunch the same way.

And these harried parents will remember someday how much fun the game was.

Living Dangerously - 2

I recently visited a big chess tournament. I competed in it last year, but this year had a busy weekend, and couldn't make it.

So I invested a few hours watching. Chess as a spectator sport? What is this?

It's more fun than you probably realize. You pick out a few games, preferably where you know the players, and follow those.

I followed one closely. A likeable young man, whom I knew as a promising youth, has grown up to become a respected master. He had Black against a very strong International Grandmaster.

Hm. Paired against a seasoned Grandmaster with the disadvantageous Black pieces. My friend Peter was up against it.

They were on Board 1, where the tournament leader plays. This table was isolated, and every move displayed on a big demonstration board. A gallery of spectators and other players taking breaks floated in and out of a bank of chairs arranged before the demonstration board.

The play is slow: lots of time spent thinking, head-shaking, grimacing. But every second you spend thinking is a second you won't have available later. Players walk around between moves, heads down, frowning.

The atmosphere writhes with tension.

This is acute pressure. Every move is potentially brilliant—or crack-brained. Wise or naive. You can win with a stunning stroke, or by accumulating tiny advantages. Or lose, ditto. Do you go for the big bopper move? Is there a trap? Will you get shown up? Ground down?

And everybody is watching.

Meanwhile on the other boards people put themselves through the same agony. Middle-aged guys like me. Teenagers. Thirty-somethings. Grade-school kids. Housewives. All ages, sizes, sexes, races, ethnic groups—all equal. It's a flat board.

All of them calculating, planning, figuring. Putting egos and wits on the line for the fun of it.

My friend Peter was working hard. He tried a bold plan against the Grandmaster, exposing a valuable but clumsy Rook in the opening to create pressure against a point in White's position. Could he get away with this? Seemed risky to me, but Peter's very tough.

The Grandmaster scowled, fretted, occasionally looked around as if he wished he were someplace else.

On another board the young North Carolina champion was defending against a blistering attack from another professional player. Elsewhere my friend Paul from Mills River was engineering a promising endgame. Another friend, Neil, was trading down to an endgame that would require impeccable technique. But Neil is much higher rated, and figured he could bring it off.

On Board 1 the Grandmaster defended the weak spot—again and again. He chipped away at Peter's forces, while Peter pressed to get his attack to work before the Grandmaster could chip too much away.

Suddenly, my friend from Mills River made a slip. His opponent could now drum up counterplay. Uh-oh.

Neil patiently looked for a breakthrough in the technical endgame, but his opponent was resourceful.

The young NC champion found an amazing defense, and suddenly had an advantage. How did he do that? Could he win?

I took notes, circulated, kept my mouth shut, fretted for my buddies, tried to figure out what they should and should not do.

Well, ultimately my side didn't have a good day.

Peter lost to a patient, brilliant defense. Paul blew the endgame, I'm afraid. Neil's opponent held him off for a draw. The young NC champion, after hours of excellent work, blundered disastrously in time trouble and got mated. Very tough.

Living dangerously takes courage. It makes your heart thump, your mouth parch, your nerves spark. All because the game is so much fun.

Living Dangerously - 3

While thinking about living dangerously recently, I heard an excellent performance of the Brahms *German Requiem*. Needless to say, this deepened my thoughts. Let me explain.

Brahms was a complicated musician. He was a careful craftsman who switched brilliantly from smooth, harmonically lush textures to complex counterpoint. He was both a barroom piano player and a scholarly, serious composer.

I've heard an entire concert of Brahms motets exploring their complex structures. You find this throughout his music: in the *German Requiem*, the movement "Wie lieblich sind deine Wohnungen" ("How lovely are thy dwelling-places") is at first smooth and placid, and suddenly explodes into a complex fugue. How do they fit together? Well, they do.

I understand Brahms was a complicated person, too, although what little I know of him is sketchy and sometimes contradictory.

For instance, I've heard him described as a devout Christian, who wanted to forge a new liturgy with this oddly titled *German Requiem*. The idea is that rather than adhering to the textual material that informs other *Requiems*, Brahms wanted something closer to his native spirit.

But I've also heard him described as a profound atheist, who used the Biblical texts not for their doctrines but for their psychological importance. They expressed powerfully the idea that life is ultimately victorious over death, and the concept that this recognition, if one can achieve it, is a source of strength and joy.

Paul Cox

I'm more interested in Brahms the artist than Brahms the theologian. It's as an artist that he seems to me to exemplify living dangerously.

Take the extremely dramatic 2nd movement of the *German Requiem,* entitled "Den alles Fleisch es ist wie Gras" ("For all flesh is as grass").

It begins with a low, threatening theme played over insistent tympani. The chorus enters, singing in stark, unharmonized octaves: "For all flesh is grass, and all the glory of man as the flower of grass." This theme recurs, becoming louder and more insistent, sounding as implacable as the fact it announces. Well sung, it is frightening.

But it's broken by lovely, lyrical passages that counsel patience and confidence, until finally—here we go—it explodes into a huge contrapuntal outcry: "Joy, everlasting joy shall be upon their heads; they shall obtain joy and gladness, and sorrow and sighing shall flee."

What impresses me about this is the uncompromising insistence on the inevitability of death on the one hand with joyful serenity on the other. How does an artist manage to stare death so firmly in the eye, and still retain the power to express this joy?

Imagine, if you can, what Brahms had to go through psychologically to internalize both of these, and artistically to find a way not only to express them with such power, but to put them together plausibly into the same structure.

Maybe from theology, maybe philosophy. But wherever the strength of will comes from, what counts is that it comes.

In a later movement, the baritone soloist sings of how "we shall all be changed in an eye-blink" (the German phrase is better: *in einem Augenblick*). Sounds threatening, but a few measures later, having recalled that "Death is swallowed up in victory," the chorus breaks again into an ecstatic celebration that becomes syncopated, even a little jazzy. You can't hear it without feeling exhilarated.

It's a thrilling moment. It defies explanation, of course, but it holds together somehow.

Brahms had the power and will to face death itself and to create from it something that makes sense in a way too deep to explain.

This is more than living dangerously. At this level it's not a game any longer.

SONGPIGS, BEARS, SKUNKS

Songpigs of North America

You've heard the little parable about teaching a pig to sing. All you get for your effort is bad music and an annoyed pig. You may think of this parable as nothing more than a pleasant lesson about futility, but I believe it is more than that. It teaches us something valuable about pigs.

Notice that in the parable, it's not the pig's fault. Pigs, you see, are not innately musical animals. They can't help it.

You will never see a beautifully illustrated coffee-table book on "Songpigs of North America." They are just not gifted in the way of vocal music.

But pigs do have other important gifts. They make fine pork and ham, and they're excellent at squealing.

In fact, I think they prefer squealing to making pork and ham. If you attempt to convert a pig into a ham, you will notice that it seeks to divert your thoughts, tries to focus your attention instead on its squealing skills.

In children's stories, pigs always have curly tails. These pigs are kind of pink and plump with innocent little faces and tails coiled as neatly as Slinky toys. Sometimes they wear little vests.

In real life, however, pigs are not quite so cute as that. They do not generally wear vests, and they are covered with coarse hair, and not in the least interested in stories that humans tell.

You saw that movie, "Babe"? Pure fiction, I can assure you.

I don't mean to disparage pigs, of course. I have nothing against them, and if you are a pig, then I wish you well. In fact, I wish you well even if you are not a pig. Unless you are some kind of tarantula, I probably wish you well.

We try to teach our children not to be like pigs. We reprimand them at table when they eat all the sweet potatoes before anyone else can get to them: "David! Stop being such a pig! I'll send you away from the table!"

(David, by the way, is perfectly content to stop and go watch some TV, having just eaten a whole bowl of sweet potatoes. But that doesn't change the moral.)

Anyway, to get back to the subject briefly, people who know tell us that pigs are unusually smart animals. Here's proof: no pig has ever written a book on aromatherapy. Pigs don't watch reality TV. Pigs don't wear neckties.

Once in high school biology, some kid brought a pig's eye to school. Our teacher asked me to cut it open, so we could see what was in it.

This was not easy, nor any fun. First, the pig insisted on watching me as I worked. Second, pig's eyes are tougher than you might think. Third, who really cares what's in there? I thought maybe a little light, like in the refrigerator, but I never found out, because I had only a dull Xacto knife to work with, and fifty minutes. So for all I know there really is a light in a pig's eye.

This, by the way, is the origin of the phrase "in a pig's eye." It refers to doubts whether there is such a light.

Some people give pigs adorable names, but this is largely in poor taste. They call them things like "Petunia" and "Lancaster." Pigs do better in this way: they call all humans "Grunt."

Anyway, I just wanted to share some thoughts and important information with you about humankind's favorite barnyard source of animal protein, except maybe the chicken.

In closing, don't play betting games with pigs. They have nothing to lose.

Our Pet Bear

Some very pleasant friends recently gave my wife and me a cat.

This cat is an ex-female who lost her tail in an accident. Her coloration is what is called tortoise-shell: dark brown with some yellow markings. She looks a little like a bear, so that's what her former family called her: Bear. So do we.

I find I enjoy the company of this cat. Seems that she and I have some traits in common.

First, we are both somewhat lazy. Bear is even lazier than I am, although I'm told that as cats go, she is about normal. She spends what seems like a lot of time asleep. I have a hunch she thinks a day is about three or four hours long.

Second, when she is awake, Bear frequently goes into research mode. She needs to check out all closets and all corners. She often asks questions, but doesn't rely on our answers.

She is a diligent observer of nature. She's kind of the Jane Goodall of yard animals. She investigates any creatures in the yard, getting pretty indignant when chipmunks appear to be making off with our acorns. My wife and I don't begrudge the chipmunks the acorns, but Bear seems to consider acorn theft a form of treachery.

This cat is friendly but reserved: she tolerates a little petting, but does not solicit it. She seems to enjoy our company, but she's unwilling to sit on people as they read.

Personally, I respect that. It's dignified. She lies on the floor nearby and alternates between looking at us and, of course, sleeping.

Paul Cox

Bear has some odd ways. She tends to come into a room and say something like "bddrp" to no one in particular. We can't figure out what "bddrp" means in cat. Probably something like "hello" in English.

Sometimes she raises her head from a quiet nap and just announces: "Bddrp," and goes back to sleep.

Another odd way of Bear is her purring. When she gets into the mood, she purrs all the time. Walks around purring. Climbs over my desk purring. Sits in the window purring.

Now, I've lived with other cats before, and I've found them to purr in times of contentment, and when giving birth. But this cat appears to forget that she is purring, and therefore forgets to turn the motor off. It's an agreeable trait, to be sure, and pleasantly odd.

For some reason she likes it when we go upstairs or downstairs. She watches, guesses where we are going, and then scurries around us to get there first. Then she tells us "bddrp."

Like most cats, Bear likes to help with deskwork. When I am trying to figure out something at the chessboard, Bear usually tries to figure it out, too. She has odd notions, however, about how the men move, and sometimes gets into violent tussles with the taller pieces.

Generally, if I wait awhile, she takes a nap, and I can think in peace.

Her helpfulness is not restricted to the chessboard. She follows my talented wife around the kitchen advising her on cooking, particularly when the dish being prepared is pizza.

Bear has definite ideas about pizza, and I think they have to do with how tangy the sauce should be. She is similarly opinionated about lemon meringue pie.

Finally, Bear is a willing helper on these columns. She is teaching me some new techniques in typing, at which she considers me abominably poor. And I think that with her help I may be able soon xdsdg6y7tttthmjnnniuollll/-=]]]]]]

Do Other Animals Have Fun?

Do other animals feel the same kind of emotions we humans feel? Can they really experience sorrow, loyalty, anger, happiness? Or is their behavior all just mindless instinct?

To some people this is as much a theological question as a biological one. If other animals feel emotions like ours, then where is human uniqueness? If our nobility flows from our emotional commitments, does it work the same for Rover, too?

If dogs, for instance, act charitably, putting another first, aren't they behaving morally? And if so, are they eligible for rewards? What about that loyal, faithful guide dog, who devotes his or her life to a blind person?

Behaving emotionally includes having fun. We could argue that if non-human creatures have real fun with real friends, then their emotional lives might be more complex and interesting than we sometimes give them credit for.

Let me tell you about some animals I knew personally.

Long ago my sterling wife and I had a funny black cat named Thurston, who moved into our apartment when he was only a few weeks old.

It was a garage apartment located in a backyard, where lived a boxer named Goliath. Goliath was aptly named: he was huge, strong, and tough-looking. Not a dog to take lightly.

Thurston was about the size of two semicolons, and Goliath about the size of a small pony. We knew that the relationship between these two would be either brief or interesting.

We let them stare at another, fascinated, through the screen door for few days. They went through a snarling period, but then they got over it, and just lay on either side of the screen looking at each other. Then one day, when all seemed peaceful, we nervously let Thurston out to play with his friend.

Goliath sniffed a few times, and Thurston looked a bit insulted. Then suddenly they rocketed off to play, chasing each other through the yard.

That became their favorite game. They played it all summer.

Goliath always let Thurston do the chasing. They tore around the yard all afternoon, Thurston waving his tiny paws ferociously and stumbling all over himself, and Goliath prancing about, dodging, jumping, barking occasionally, not getting too far ahead, acting silly but never rough. Sometimes we would see Goliath jumping around with Thurston hanging from his neck like Tarzan's Boy. When they got tired, they lay together in the shade and rested. Thurston didn't appear to enjoy getting licked.

They made a comical sight—two unlikely buddies playing in the sun. Of course, both had to know it was a game. Goliath could have devoured Thurston as an appetizer at any moment, but he was invariably playful. For Thurston's part, if he weren't absolutely certain it was a game, he would never have messed with such a big critter. Somehow they both knew.

As the summer wore on, Thurston got bigger, more agile, and stronger. The game changed a little, but they remained the best of friends, and when we moved away, we knew that Thurston missed his giant buddy.

Now, was this friendly play, or mindless instinctual behavior? Were they like human friends, with the commitment and unselfishness we associate with friendship? Or were they just insensibly being dumb animals?

Here's what I think. I have as much reason to respect the emotional lives of these two animals as I have to respect the emotional life of anyone else I know. If they weren't committed friends having a whale of a lot of fun together, then I don't know who is.

If that's a theological statement, well, OK. It makes sense to me.

Getting To Know The Bear

My conversational wife and I were at dinner, when we heard an odd noise in the yard. No big deal, hey? We thought little of it; nothing unusual about a noisy yard.

After dinner, as I was cleaning up, my wife suddenly came running in, all a-jabber. "Window! Now! It's! Go! Oh, my! Hurry!" and so on like that, she said.

So I ran to the window and "what to my wondering eyes should appear" but a big black bear. Well, it nearly rhymes.

He (or she, in case it matters) had a thistle feeder down from a pole, and was licking it. Looked pretty foolish, as a matter of fact.

I went downstairs to a closer window, grabbed a camera, and snapped a couple of pictures. My wife, meanwhile, called our neighbor, with whom we share a yard, jabbering and exclaiming as described above. She seemed a bit excited.

Then she picked up our cat—coincidentally named "Bear"—and held her up to the window. Bear saw the bear and immediately remembered some important business under the bed.

After awhile our woolly guest, annoyed by my picture taking, loped off. He seemed to think it was a shame a fellow can't even take a quiet lick off a thistle feeder nowadays.

That was that, except that he must have come back later, because next morning the whole feeder pole was lying on the ground.

So that's the big adventure. Not quite enough to dine out on, but fun for a conversation. Particularly so since none of my pictures came out. In the absence of evidence to the contrary I am free to grow the bear to any size I need at the moment, and even to interpolate additional bears into the scene if I wish.

I even considered introducing a lion in one re-telling of the story, but then decided I wouldn't get away with it.

Actually, what most people don't know about this story is that I have been researching this bear. What kind of bear is it? What are its tastes, its views on important issues? As a concerned American, I wanted to know.

I was unable to ascertain, for instance, whether it was a Democrat or a Republican. Might even have been a Libertarian, judging from his direct, unsubtle approach to our bird feeders. I don't think he was a Nader partisan, but I'm not sure why. Looked if anything more of a Buchanan type.

So I list him as either a-political or perhaps Buchananist, if there is such a word.

In the matter of religion I was similarly unable to get a good fix. I listened closely for any Bible quotations it might have used before dining on the thistles, but heard nothing. At least, while it was licking thistles, it was not citing scripture. And I don't fault him for that: many good people lick their thistles in silence.

I queried whether he was a pagan, but got only a red-eyed stare for my trouble. I thought he might have felt insulted. When I asked its position on transubstantiation—usually a pretty good index of church affiliation—he scratched himself thoughtfully, but without making any clear commitment.

I had to put him down as, let us say, un-churched. But if anyone has evidence to the contrary, I can be persuaded.

My inquiries went on and on. Free-trader? Pro-Life? Pro-Choice? Home-Schooler? Flat Tax? Evolutionist? Creationist? Atlanta Braves fan?

Tell you the truth, I don't think that this bear took much of a position on any of the important issues of the day.

It must be nice.

How Lazy My Cat Is

We recently put a screened porch, or "scream porch" if you prefer, on the back of our house.

Our lumpy, funny cat Bear thinks it is pretty fine.

Even when the weather is chilly, even when rain is blowing in through the screen, she wants to be out there. This is because she has important work to do.

She has discovered a colony of treacherous chipmunks. Some of the malapert little scoundrels bustle right up to the porch and wiggle their noses at her!

Bear crouches in ready mode, and the closer the chipmunk gets, the readier she becomes. Eventually she is twitching all over with excitement. Her ears are focused, her haunches coiled, her eyes intent.

And sometimes she forgets where she is, and makes a sudden leap for the chipmunk, conking her head against the screen.

Well, it doesn't really hurt, I think, but she gets embarrassed, and scowls at the chipmunks for a time. She clearly blames her embarrassment on them, and plots her revenge.

But her plans get too complicated, and her attention wanders.

Over to the bird feeder, where some alarmingly yellow finches are grocery shopping.

Bear is astonished at their effrontery. But then a small club of wild turkeys comes poking around talking quietly among themselves about whatever it is turkeys are interested in. Bear is fascinated: how did something as silly looking as that ever get into her yard, anyway?

And so her morning goes. Bear carefully monitors the yard for us, her vigilance never faltering. She's on duty.

Well, except when she finds a little plastic thing on the floor that she can pick up and pretend to chew. But it jumps out of her mouth! And skitters across the floor!

And when she pounces on it, it flips away, and she has to chase it, with all the acrobatics she can dream up.

Sometimes she does somersaults over it. This rascally plastic thing requires some effort, but eventually she quells it.

It makes into a busy morning. She gets worn out, and puddles herself in a sunny spot for a quiet nap.

Afternoon is more of the same, and when my wife and I repair to the porch for an appetizer, Bear is amazed that it should be dinnertime already. She looks at us in wonder: what do you two think you are doing? she wants to know.

In the evening she sometimes watches TV with the aforesaid wife and me, but most evenings she is pretty worn out by her back-porch duty, and loses herself in a profound slumber, oblivious of anything Niles Crane might have to say.

I think about this. Watching critters, jumping about with a little plastic toy, taking naps. Fetching a drink of water from time to time. What kind of life is this?

How lazy can an animal get?

But then I ask myself: what must she think of me? I sit and stare at a big piece of paper every morning while I eat a bagel. I sit and stare at my computer. I sit and stare at a book. I move chess pieces around a piece of wood. Sometimes I get in the car and drive away, but then I come back.

And then my wife and I eat salted nuts on her porch.

And we mew at one another all day long, or pick up the phone and mew into that.

She must think we're crazy.

So there you have it. I think she's lazy, and she probably thinks I'm crazy.

Still, we get along pretty well anyway. Just don't show her this.

Our Wild Life With The Wildlife

When we moved into our house, kind of in the woods, a man helping us move said we should see a lot of wildlife. You bet, I said, and animals, too.

We thought that was funny at the time. Maybe I'm revising that view.

Now, we've had the usual squirrels, chipmunks, deer, birds, turkeys, foxes. Nice visitors.

I've mentioned before about a bear who came into our yard. It came to do several tasks: wreck bird feeders, discombobulate my impressionable wife, scare the starch out of our cat, and expose me for an inept photographer.

At least, I assume that was the bear's agenda, because that is what it accomplished, rather efficiently.

Recently another bear visited. Apparently it came several times one day. My wife found it at one point out on the deck, looking in like a kid outside a candy store. She actually got pictures.

Well, they might have been pictures of a bear, or else out-of-focus shots of a Franklin stove. But she definitely photographed something black and furry out on the deck.

Incidentally, the bear once again frightened Bear (our cat) out of her wits. She walked around saucer-eyed for several days, flinching and staring wildly toward the deck. I don't think she slept more than about fifteen hours a day.

Recently we had another visitor. I looked up one day to see a mother skunk and three little skunklings waddling across the yard.

They were undeniably cute little fellers, although their mother seemed to me somewhat impatient with them. Instead of positive feedback and time-outs, she preferred open-handed discipline.

This made me nervous, because if I have to have skunks, I want well-adjusted, happy, unflappable skunks.

Anyway, these fur units lumbered and sniffed across the yard, and, to my horror, made directly for the porch where I was sitting.

Oh no, I thought. Don't tell me they've moved in with us. Don't tell me these are my new roommates.

I told my wife what I'd seen, and we reviewed our options.

All viable options started with the principle of keeping the skunks really happy.

Could we bar access to the under-porch region? Good idea, but only if we are certain no one is at home.

Could we somehow encourage them to seek other quarters? Not without risking rudeness.

We decided to wait a day or two: maybe they don't really live here. And sure enough, after a couple of visits, they disappeared. Maybe there's no crisis.

Except that this morning I went out to get my paper, and walked—as I often do—through an invisible cobweb. I brushed it away, but had the sense I hadn't quite completed the task.

All morning, I found myself harvesting little strands of web from my whiskers, from my ears, from my eyebrows.

And finally, at an afternoon concert during which I was constantly fooling with my head (not an attractive spectacle, you know), I finally found a tiny symmetrical spider fleeing down my arm. He had been residing on my head all day, I suppose, trying to squirt enough web to catch me.

OK: this has gone far enough.

Now, I know a bit about mitochondria and the little mites that live in human eyebrows and the host of other nano-creatures that share our bodies with us. That I'm used to.

But bears and skunks and spiders inviting themselves to live on intimate terms with us? I don't so much care for that. At least I want a vote on it.

We are not alone, you see. And sometimes I wish we were maybe a little aloner.

Introducing What's Her Name

My adroit wife and I have decided to share our—and Bear's—home with another cat. There are adjustments to be made for all of us.

The first thing to settle was the problem of a name.

The former host of this cat called her "Pumpkin." And it's not a bad name. She's an autumnally-hued creature. Dark yellow, red, brown, and so on, like a pile of leaves with eyes. Kind of a color-reversal of Bear.

But the name Pumpkin just isn't exactly satisfactory. It's a name for a human child, when properly shortened to "Punkin'." Not quite right for a cat. We had a problem to solve.

Now I have what I believe to be the infallible method for determining the correct name of a house pet. You just look at the creature and some word will pop into your head. This is probably the right name for the pet.

This method worked beautifully with our first cat, a short-haired black warrior, whom we named Thurston. My wife used the method to name our second cat, a long-haired white female, whom she called Wife. No one ever doubted that those were the names registered for those animals in the big name registry in the sky.

So I looked at this new cat and immediately found her correct name: "Humidor." It's not that she looks particularly like a place to store cigars, but that the dark, colorful word itself seems appropriate to her.

I figured we could shorten this, in extremity, to "Dora" or "Dory," and on formal occasions address her with the full "Humidor."

My views were confirmed when Bear and this cat first met. Bear immediately said: "H!" I assumed this to be short for "Humidor," and was pleased.

I told my wife about "Humidor," and said I had dismissed the other candidate names I had processed, "Alert" and "Trim-line."

She was not persuaded. She favored "Girlfriend," since one of our motives in inviting this cat to live with us was to provide Bear a companion.

We had several conversations on this subject, all inconclusive. Or you could say we went a round or two over it.

But then my wife had an idea. "What about 'Owl'?"

Now, she may be onto something there, I have to admit. In fact, I think the new cat and Bear may have had the same conversation, because as soon as Bear said "H!" the new cat replied "Owl!" And to think I missed that!

And they've been having this same conversation ever since. One says "H!" and the other says "Owl!" (Did we give Bear the wrong name? Maybe she's really H.)

This has become a game with them by now: they chase one another around the house having a grand time turning over things, hiding behind doors and pouncing, jumping, and then touching noses just to make sure it's all in play.

So I guess Humidor has been renamed. She is Owl, and I have to get used to it. But it's tough: whenever I speak to her I can't remember "Owl," and wind up calling her: "Whatever the heck your name is." I don't think she cares, though.

Anyway, I have salvaged something from the ruins of my endeavor to name the cat Humidor. Here's what I've salvaged: a new reflex test for physicians.

You know how a physician taps your knee and your foot jumps? Or taps your forearm in the right place, and your finger pops up?

Well, I propose that a physician could just look a patient in the eye and say: "I've decided to name my cat 'Humidor'." A normal patient's eyebrows will invariably rise.

The Great Plot Against Or Maybe On Behalf Of Humans

I'm sorry to alarm you, but I think you should be aware of this.

The other morning I was fixing myself a little breakfast—a bagel, some juice, a little pot of Darjeeling.

Our sweet-tempered, lumpy cat, Bear, was with me, and I became aware that she was observing everything I did very carefully. Her head swiveled with my every motion, her facial expression studious. She was focused, I realized, on learning how to do this. At one point she asked a question: "Eeu?"

"Well," I said. "You boil water, and then pour it in this pot with the leaves, see. Like this."

"Eeu," she said.

"I don't think you would, either, but I like it. I'm a person, after all."

Later as I reflected, I began to realize what was going on. I was being studied.

Bear refuses to discuss this with me, and her refusal confirms my suspicious. I am convinced that the other animals, the ones over whom we think we have dominion, are watching us, learning from us, and they have a strategy.

I don't know how they coordinate, but then, I believe they don't know why I put pieces of paper into the mailbox every morning, or how that newspaper gets there, which I stare at as I eat the bagel and drink the tea.

But they clearly are coordinated, just as I clearly have some reason for staring at the morning paper.

I think I'm beginning to understand, though.

Cats have the assignment to dope out how we do things around the house. How we cook. How we work in the office, what the keys on our computer keyboard mean. What we are doing with these odd-looking things on the chessboard.

"Our" Bear watches TV with us, learning about things like e-commerce and fashionable yet casual clothing.

The dogs' task is to follow us around outside and to get us to reveal useful tidbits of information. I suspect that by now, dogs know as much about agriculture as most humans do, and a good bit about rifles and pickup trucks.

I wondered about bugs, until I thought about home construction. Yes, yes, that's it: imagine what a verbal ant or roach could tell you about how houses are built. Not just in broad outline, either, but in exquisite detail. They have to know it.

I don't know much about the assignments of the other creatures. I rather guess deer are along to assure that all the other animals are properly treated, like Human Resources professionals, and clearly crows have the job of making sure everybody is on the job early each morning. I hear them every day cussing out some poor soul or other who must have missed an assignment.

So while I haven't worked out all the details, I am pretty sure I have a good general idea what is going on. At some point a signal will be given. We might not be aware of it, but the other animals will. They will have pooled all the knowledge of us that they have collected, and they will take over.

What can you do?

I would suggest you just have a warm breakfast and go along with it.

So the moose is in charge for a few thousand years. Maybe a badger will run Microsoft, or a nice horse will take charge of the Department of the Interior.

How bad can it be, anyway?

My view is that if we have been reasonably kind to these guys, they'll treat us well.

I can't imagine that old Bear would let anybody hurt us. Relax.

Deer and Table Manners

We put out a bird feeder near the ground. Figured we would accommodate the birds that like to take meals down low, and we were willing to put up with squirrels. Once you accept squirrels in your heart, they really are kind of cute, you know.

The birds enjoyed the feeder. Crows squawked about it, doves prissed around it, cardinals looked important as their mates fed. Juncos jumped around, blue jays made announcements, and there was plenty to go around.

The squirrels kept up a circus, along with the chipmunks. There was always a bustle, everyone having fun, taking turns, cracking bird jokes, tricking one another. It was like a daily backyard multi-species picnic.

Then along came some deer.

Now, deer are attractive animals. They seem to have a calm, stately dignity to them, and they've learned good poses from Walt Disney.

These deer helped themselves to the birds' luncheons, and soon the birds had to line up behind the squirrels, who were waiting for the deer to finish.

Something seemed a little out of kilter.

Then we naively decided to put out some shrubbery beside the house. We thought this would give us a civilized, flowery border.

What looked like a shrubbery border to us looked like a salad bar to the deer.

But my benevolent wife took a shine to these deer, especially one doe who visits our yard with a little speckled fawn. The mother takes her meal while the little one dashes here and chases there getting excited about bugs and breezes. There's no doubt, the critter is really cute, and the pair is appealing.

There's also a buck whose antlers are growing nicely, fuelled, of course, by our corn. Well, I don't begrudge him. He's got to live too, you know.

You can see what's coming, I suspect. We now have our own little floating herd of deer, who seem to consider that we are camping in their cafeteria. These deer sometimes quarrel with each other, sometimes play around, sometimes eat our bushes. In a graceful and dignified way, of course.

They seem to get irked if we sit on our deck. The does look stern and stamp their front feet. I am reminded of a girl I knew in the second grade, who stamped like that. She often got red in the face, stamped her foot, and hollered "I mean it now!"

The deer are daintier than she was, but it is clearly the same idea.

The bucks also have their gestures. I noticed one recently standing by the empty feeder (guess how it got that way). He was glaring at our back door, imperiously lifting his chin. The message was clear: "Get out here right now, lady! Make it quick! HONGRY!"

My question is: what kind of table manners have we come to tolerate around here?

When our kids were little we had none of that. When a kid insisted on a cookie, and we thought he or she didn't need it, there was no cookie. End of story.

There were battles over our policies, but our course was clear. And the kids turned out well.

But these deer are getting uncomfortably rude. Greedy. Demanding. Boorish.

When the deer become impolite, what do we do? Explain? Nope. Send them to bed without supper? Not so easy. Spank them? You go first.

So their demands get more and more urgent, and our supply gets more and more expensive.

At last, though, I have a plan. Next week I'm going to put out some signs that say "CHEAP VENISON."

That ought to do the trick.

An Update And A Philosophical Query

Some have asked about the family of skunks that seems to be summering under our porch. Here's a report.

Periodically an adult female skunk waddles across the yard. Her goal appears to be a conversation with our cat, Bear, who maintains an observation post on the back porch.

Bear complains, however, that all the skunk wants to do is ask questions, and moreover, that she tends to ask the same question over and over.

Now, I can't understand much of what Bear tells me about this, because she tends to doze off in mid-sentence, even in mid-syllable, unless I scratch her ears. And then when I do, she loses her train of thought and begins rumbling instead of making sense.

But I think the gist of these interrogatory sessions is something like this:

"Are the people who live here pretty nice?" Bear says she answers yes.

"Is there anything around here to eat?" Bear, of course, has three squares a day for free, so she doesn't understand the question very well.

"Have you seen my little ones anywhere?" Bear says she answers no.

And that is pretty much it. Skunks, as I have said, are cute creatures, but a little empty-headed.

But why not? It doesn't take much brains to succeed as a skunk. Think about it.

Paul Cox

The bear (not our cat, but a real bear) hasn't been around lately. This bear seems not to need our company much, and that is fine by Bear (the cat).

As for me, I kind of enjoy the excitement of a visit from the bear. Something about long, careless claws, I guess. But this bear really does mangle our bird-feeding hardware pretty badly, so I am willing for it or him or her to come infrequently. A matter of the expense, you know.

Deer continue to saunter around our yard, looking regal. They pretend just to be in the neighborhood on their way to visit someone more important.

But of course, if we do happen to have something growing in the lawn that we would like them to sample, they're willing just to take a taste or so and let us know whether we are on the right track.

I'm not fooled by this hauteur, however, because they often have little ones with them, who give away the game.

A fawn is as taken with people as a stately buck is disdainful. They are skittish, however, and don't have much attention span. Let a cloud move over the sun and they'll sense disaster and dash for the bush. While the buck continues to look down on us superciliously.

Heck, I don't care about them. I'm not impressed. I once met the governor.

Do you suppose that deer and cats and bears and skunks spend as much time trying to think of us in terms of themselves as we spend trying to think of them in terms of ourselves?

I mean, do deer think of humans as oddly-shaped deer who put cloth all over ourselves in the morning to hide our lack of natural handsome coats?

Does our cat, Bear, think we are just too high-strung to get the normal 18 hours of sleep a day? Does she think we are demented, looking at a book or a TV for several hours at a stretch? (She may be right, I'm afraid.)

Does the skunk think we are just stupid not to notice that she is using our backyard as a resort?

Well, they probably do.

They're probably chuckling over us in their equivalent of our newspaper right now.

And why not? We're just as silly as anybody else, after all.

NATURE AND THE SEASONS

What To Do When It's Winter Outdoors

'Tis the season to be jolly. That's the first thing about winter that you need to remember: be jolly.

I don't think it matters whether you are jolly during other seasons. But in winter you are cooped up indoors with people, some of whom you know. Jolly-ness is therefore essential.

You don't want to go outside, because you will slip on ice, fall, and have a sore patch on your knee for weeks.

So here's the ideal indoor program for a cold, jolly, snowy winter weekend morning when outside looks like an overturned paperweight.

Get up late and build a fire. Make some hot chocolate and cinnamon buns. Get out a jigsaw puzzle, and put some good music on—something interesting and a little jolly.

Tell the little kids they can stay in their footy pajamas all day. Plan to play as a family with the jigsaw puzzle before the fire, sipping your hot chocolate. Figure on tickling the kids from time to time.

See? It's the ideal life, just like in a TV commercial. Really jolly.

Of course, there are a few issues you will need to deal with.

First, there is the matter of jolly firewood. It is outdoors, so someone must get it. This involves putting on actual clothing, including something to protect your feet from snow.

But this won't work: jolly snow will get into your shoes no matter what you do. Even if you wear hip boots, snow will get in. Might as well go out barefoot, except that your concerned wife will nag you to wear shoes.

So you get some firewood, which is probably wet and mostly rotten and full of jolly bugs anyway. But you have it.

To make the fireplace work you need something for kindling. Something like yesterday's newspaper, which is a little wet from being out on the porch in the jolly recycling bin. But you get it, and bunch up several pages.

Matches? Someplace or other around here. Honey, can you find me some matches?

Arrange the soggy logs above the frozen newspaper, leaving space for the jolly air to move around—very important. Use five or six matches, because they go out before anything catches.

Use five or six more when the first light dies too early. You will burn yourself at least once.

Finally the paper catches, and sets up a nice, jolly, red, hard-working flame. A smoky flame. Your wife will shout, and you will remember to open the jolly flue.

Should you open a window to let the jolly smoke out and the snow in? Or instead just put up with it for awhile? There will be a jolly disagreement over this.

Meanwhile, there isn't any cocoa to make hot chocolate with. Will jolly onion soup do?

Also, no cinnamon bun fixings: how about peanut butter and jolly jelly?

The kids are full of life and pep. They want to watch cartoons on TV, while tearing paper into jolly little pieces. Why do kids do that? Why don't they want to play with a jigsaw puzzle? Who are these kids?

And where's the card table, anyway? Why can't a guy set up a jigsaw puzzle around here, for goodness' sake?

You wife doesn't answer, because she has started a big load of jolly laundry.

Besides, your feet are wet and cold, and your burned finger hurts, and the house stinks of wet newspaper smoke. Bah.

Well, there's some jolly work you needed to get done anyway. Oh, boy.

Jolly, you see, ain't really all that easy. Not unless you live in a song somewhere.

The Return of Spring

Before long the cold, wet stump of winter will be gone. The soggy ground will firm up, the mists will clear away, and spring will hit us like a sudden dawn.

Sunshine will pour down like honey from the sky. Dogwoods and wild cherries, having been around for several weeks already, will float gentle clouds of color and light through the woods.

Pansies and tulips and daffodils, tucked against the sides of houses, will giggle together over pretty little jokes about squirrels and chipmunks.

Hummingbirds will zoom around on important missions, sticking their noses into everything, staging dogfights above flower patches.

Finches will be alarming lemon-yellow, and cardinals red as blood, and jays cool and jaunty like middle managers in pale blue polyester suits.

Robins will pop around the yard looking for worms in the soft dirt. Robins feel proprietary about spring: they think they cause it.

Crows, however, liked the raw, ugly late winter weather, so they holler and squawk: "It'll be ba-a-a-ack!" Nobody takes them seriously, though.

Kids will walk around in baggy shorts and tight skin, and we old guys will walk around just the other way.

People will smile a little more, and linger on the sidewalk or on lawns to chat a minute with each other in the sunlight.

Golfers will get serious about their golf, and baseball people will remember what life was supposed to be all about.

Fishermen will breathe a little easier. Fish won't.

Hikers will hit the trails, with sturdy shoes and floppy hats and sticks. They'll find the elusive flowers, pause at the busy streams, and listen for unfamiliar birdcalls.

Iced tea season will come around again. Sweet or unsweetened? A little lemon is nice, and a sprig of mint.

Set a big clear glass jar of tea and cold water on the porch in the morning, and it will be perfect at lunchtime.

Lunchtime will involve tomato sandwiches, cut thick, with mayonnaise and a little salt. Want some basil on that, maybe a sprinkle of Parmesan? Not a bad idea with your iced tea. You can have a little cookie for dessert about once or twice a week, but don't overdo it.

Late afternoons will hold the day's warmth a little longer, so we can sit on the porch with a neighbor and make meaningless, friendly talk as day fades.

Eventually our words will hang still in the dark of early evening, but we won't want to go in. Even if it's a little chilly yet, there is a kind of vitamin in the spring air that makes us feel good.

Maybe we'll fire up the grill. Ribs? Salmon? A tender little roasting chicken? Why not? It's nice out.

Churches and clubs will hold picnics on the lawn, with plates of fried chicken, deviled eggs, hushpuppies, casseroles, salads, cakes, brownies. How do they know what to bring? I don't think there is overt planning, but the menu is always the same, and it's the perfect picnic menu.

As June approaches, younger kids begin to smell water: summer vacation is coming. Classes and lessons creep on forever, trudging from point to point as the kids' blood rushes in anticipation of that grand moment when they burst free of school.

Remember how that felt? On that first day of vacation and last day of school the world seems endless, brilliant, warm, free, and open. The sensation lasts for only a little while, but it's worth waiting a year for.

Spring will happen. Trust me: gray and wet and cold as the late winter seems, spring will always come.

That's a promise.

Thoughts On The End of Summer

When I was young, I didn't like the end of summer. Others seemed to, but not me. I thought any day in which I couldn't get hot in the sun was a day when I had been defrauded.

I knew that the end of summer meant the beginning of autumn. School. Chilly weather. Shoes every day. A cold bathroom floor.

There were, of course, pleasures to late summer. The tobacco markets opened in late or middle August, for instance.

Everyone went to the warehouses and strolled about. There was a bustle and purpose to it that may happen only in farming towns at harvest time.

Lines of men, often in white shirts with frantic wide ties, walked intently along rows of waist-high piles of tobacco in the sales warehouses. The tobacco was stacked neatly on pallets: huge, beautiful golden leaves tied into bundles, fragrant and soft. The farmers were proud of their crops, and had clearly taken trouble to show off their tobacco.

Ahead of the line of buyers, an auctioneer walked slowly, chanting his hypnotic babble, punctuated with shouts of "Sold!" An earnest man followed right behind him, instantly calculating the price of each pile of leaves, writing on the tickets, never making a mistake in his complicated arithmetic.

Elsewhere, high school football players struggled and sweated, and then showed up in the drugstore after practice, looking hugely fatigued, ready to accept adulation. Our local militia, ready to defend our town against footballers from other towns wearing colors we thought were a little inferior to our red and white.

Trees began dropping their leaves. Soon there were huge mounds of oak leaves, and sullen kids my age with rakes flipping the leaves around aimlessly, wishing they were playing marbles instead. Smaller kids jumping in the piles of raked leaves.

School supplies in the five-and-dime: rulers, paste, pads of lined paper, protractors, lunchboxes, binders, stacks of pencils.

And eventually, as I got older, these images won me over. I began to see that as the time for the indolent play of summer closed, a new time began. It wasn't just a season ending, but another season re-starting, as well.

Like summer, autumn would have its rhythms and its activities, and then would reach its climax in the complex holiday season. Halloween would come, and then, just we were getting over Halloween, Thanksgiving, and right on that, Christmas.

Of course, to a kid, any Christmas seems impossibly far off. In late August, Christmas is like heaven—a wonderful thing to think about, but too far away to be a reality just yet.

It takes years to mature into an understanding of the full logic and rhythm of the year. You have to live through it a few times to understand how the end of summer implies the eventual end of autumn, the onset of winter, even the awakening of spring—and then another summer.

You have to reach a certain age before you begin to realize that summer doesn't really end and then later, begin again. Nor autumn, nor Thanksgiving and Christmas, nor anything that holds a place in the cycle of time.

And once you begin to realize that, your understanding of it deepens over the years. Nothing ever really ends. Nothing ever really starts from scratch. What we do this year grows out of what we did last year.

A lifetime is a continuum, not a set of segments. A ribbon, not a string of pearls. A single moment that turns different colors as the light changes.

Childhood, like summer, never really ends. It just grows up a little.

The Seasons of Beginning

I used to know some people in the catalog merchandizing business. For them, there are two seasons of the year: fall and spring. In that order.

I believe that conception shows considerable wisdom.

We all know in our hearts that the year begins sometime in September. The kids get new clothes and fresh notebooks with clean paper. School starts, and football militias begin their yearly campaigns on behalf of their constituencies. Cooler air brings a renewal of energy.

Automobile dealers and opera companies and charities all know to start the year in the fall.

Churches reassemble their members and celebrate homecoming. Householders look to their furnaces and their firewood. Even the trees drop their used leaves, and people drive in the country to see the colors, so vivid you can nearly hear them. The earth discovers its beauty again, and aggressively reasserts it.

I think that deep inside, fall brings us a sense of starting, of cleaning house and getting our lives underway again.

The Day of Atonement comes at the right time of the year—a time of taking stock and cleansing.

Fall is the season when we have to assure that we will make it through winter. It is the season when we check in with our friends and family to be sure all are provisioned and prepared. Between Labor Day and Thanksgiving (for Americans, anyway) we ready ourselves for the year ahead.

Fall is planning, ordering, review. It is a season of laying-by, and of getting ready. Do you have a warm jacket? Better check, before you need it.

Bears fatten themselves not because summer is over, but because winter is going to start soon. They sense their annual sleepiness starting.

Fall is the time when farmers decide what to plant next year, where to plant it, and how to pay for it. Fall is the time when the next year begins, just as the last one ends.

And oddly, what we are planning and preparing for is another season of beginning. Spring is the affirmation that we were right when we lay provisions by in the fall. Just as in fall we harvest what we planted in spring, so in spring we see the fruits of autumn preparations.

Fall and spring are complementary seasons, when people begin different phases of the great cycles of our lives.

Fall is crispness; spring is softness. Fall is a cool breeze; spring is warm sunlight. Fall is review; spring is awakening. Fall is a celebration of maturity and readiness; spring a celebration of youth and promise.

Fall is the season of flames; spring the season of flowers.

I believe we human beings need the seasons. We need our cycles: day and night, prosperity and trouble, sickness and health. We gripe about them, of course, but I don't think life would be right without them.

I read about a place near Chicago that guarantees 72-degree weather, indoors or out, all through the year. The idea is that you retire to this place and never feel discomfort again.

I don't know how they do it, and I don't want to find out. A life without brisk autumn winds? A life without the little shy smile of sunlight on a chilly March afternoon? A life without the first snowfall of November? Thanksgiving at 72 degrees? Easter at 72 degrees?

No thanks, not for me. I need the seasons. I need the occasional bite of change and readjustment.

I need fall and spring to tell me, over and over and over, that life on this planet is always about starting over again.

Gardens and Mazes

My friend Ernie Mills told me recently about a maze being constructed by the Brevard College Garden Club. We even toured the site of the maze.

It's a natural combination, gardens and mazes. Both are full of symbolic importance, for our own culture and many others.

No room here to go into all the magic of gardens. Today is about mazes.

A maze replicates some of the most important processes of life, as we try to choose a cunningly concealed path to the end. We meander along, get lost, lose track of how we got where we are, retrace the same false paths over and over.

Sooner or later, of course, we reach the end, and realize when we do that we're a little sorry, because the fun is all over. Overcoming frustrations, enjoying the challenge, and—if the maze is in a garden—enjoying the place itself.

It has a lot to do with being human, of course, with recognizing at some point before it's all over that what matters is how we go about figuring things out along the way.

I thought about building a maze. It seems to me there are several ways to do it.

I'm afraid I'd go about it in the wrong way. I'd be tempted to start with graph paper.

I'd draw up a plan. I'd chart my maze, being careful to include plenty of false paths, making certain that false and true paths would intersect in enough places to be bewildering.

But not too bewildering. I'd build in some encouragements along the way, to counter the discouragements.

I'd plot how fast a person walks in a place like that. Assuming that a person, given a simple binary choice, will usually choose wrong about half the time, I'd work out just how long it would take the average person to solve my maze.

Then I could apply this information, see, to perfecting my design. I'd know before I ever picked up a shovel just how many people could enjoy my maze at any time, how long they would be in there, how many minutes I should allow between visitors, and so on.

I could derive metrics from this, and know in advance pretty much all I needed to know about my maze.

In fact, I wouldn't even really need to build the maze at all. I'd have all the data without it. I'd have solved the maze problem before I started.

Well, that's one good way to go about it. But I think it's the wrong good way.

Here's a better way.

What if we go instead to the site first and look it over? We get an idea for an interesting path, and open that path up. Maybe the path seems good for a while, but eventually we realize it's not going to get us conveniently to the end.

So we set up a little bench and take a breather. Maybe we can sit and read a few minutes before resuming our job.

Then we go back a little way, and sure enough, we spy another good place for a path. Hm. We start clearing that one, and see what happens. . . .

And someday we will probably have built a maze. Maybe not: maybe all we will build is a pleasant place in the woods where we can walk around, sit on a shady bench from time to time and read a little, or maybe watch some birds or chipmunks go about their own lives.

Oh, heck, here we are talking about gardens after all. But maybe that's OK, too.

The Big Bang

Back in the middle forties when I was young, six or seven I guess, we lived in an old parsonage with a tin roof. My brother and I shared a bedroom upstairs. Sometimes as we slept, rain would patter onto that tin roof and trickle down the windows, making our sleep sweet and deep.

Where we lived was a little scary, actually. Our father's church was next door, a dark old building that seemed to me at that age to be full of mysterious hallways and unexpected doors, and alive with creaks and croaks and footsteps of invisible people.

Behind the church (and behind our house) was an old church graveyard with ancient graves, some dating from long before the Civil War. We preferred not to think much about that.

Next door a neighbor owned most of the rest of the block, and it was overgrown into a dense thicket. To a kid like me, that seemed like a dark and impenetrable forest. Were there bears?

Around our house were big trees—oaks, pines, and walnuts—that contributed to an atmosphere of darkness and even gloom.

Sometimes at night acorns would fall off the oak trees. They hit the roof with a little snap, and kind of skipped down the roof saying PADUCAH-PADUCAH-PADUCAH, accelerating as they went.

And sometimes walnuts would fall off. These would hit the roof with a healthy WHACK, and then roll their way down, BOOGLE-BOOGLE-BOOGLE. They were even more fun than the acorns.

Sleeping in this upstairs bedroom was an ongoing adventure and a treat for the ears.

One night in late summer, however, a thunderstorm blew up.

Paul Cox

Now, of course, like most southeastern towns, we had plenty of summer thunderstorms. But this one was unusually severe, and unusually close. The wind wailed, rain cascaded down the roof, and a steady salvo of acorns and walnuts fired at us.

It was an exciting night of bangs and lights, and we were having a fine time. Slightly scary, but that was part of the fun.

Then a particular bolt of lightening, maybe lost and separated from the rest of the storm, struck.

It would be useless for me try to imitate the sound. You'll have to imagine it. First see the flash, as for an instant the whole bedroom lit up in that spooky reverse light that lightening brings.

At the same instant imagine a huge, overwhelming cracking noise. But don't forget to imagine the urgent FIZZ that happens when lightening strikes nearby. Just for an instant, it was clearly the end of the world.

Where the lightening struck, we later learned, was the walnut tree. It split off a huge branch, loaded with walnuts, onto our house.

So the ear-splitting crack of the lightening was immediately followed by another crash as that heavy walnut branch landed on the roof and dismissed all its walnuts to roll, bounce, jolt, and otherwise tumble down the roof.

If we thought the lightening strike was the end of the world, the crash of the walnut tree confirmed our suspicions. Not only was the world coming to an end, but also most of the sky was obviously falling upon our house.

My mother was heard to holler, "What was that!"

My brother and I responded differently. We had been learning an excellent vocabulary of forbidden words, which we took this opportunity to rehearse. I think our father may have responded similarly.

Next day we surveyed the scene: twisted wood, broken limbs, a dent in the roof. Cleanup took days.

But the main effect was the memory of the experience: an instant of noise and light, followed by maybe thirty seconds of the house threatening to fall down.

All in all, it was much more fun than a birthday party.

The Bird Club

When I was young, my family lived in a parsonage in a small town in eastern North Carolina. Next door was an empty lot, and beside that a dark old house.

The lady in this house was several hundred years old, I guessed. She lived alone, and the story was that she had been married once to an important Italian prince. Her name was an alarming mixture of crotchety English and prickly Italian.

We were, of course, afraid of her.

I'm not going to give you her name, because this story is not really about her as she was—a perfectly pleasant, gracious person, I later learned. But at the time she seemed dark and terrible, and that imaginary terrible person is who this is about.

Behind her house was a large, overgrown lot. It looked to me and my playmates like a jungle.

This jungle harbored important wildlife. Certainly wild dogs and wild boars. Bears. There were lively reports of panthers, and huge snakes with insides larger than our outsides.

The lady herself was also scary. She seldom spoke to us kids, but mostly looked fierce.

Then one summer this lady founded The Bird Club.

The Bird Club was open to boys of a certain age. I don't remember exactly, but eight seems about right. My brother was eligible; I was not.

Now, membership in The Bird Club was not optional. If you were of age, you were a member. Period. Your mother dressed you in clean shorts at 10:00 on Saturday morning, and you went.

Usually, you waited until you saw a friend headed that way: few elected to arrive alone.

My brother told me what they did at The Bird Club. First, there was some stuff about birds, with pictures. Then they had refreshments. Then they ran around and played, and then it was time to come home. He seemed to think it wasn't so bad.

I was mystified. Wasn't the place haunted? What about the jungle? The wild dogs? The snakes?

My brother attended The Bird Club most Saturday mornings that summer, and I became more and more curious.

I became eligible to join at my birthday that August, and walked shakily next door one Saturday with my brother. My heart was pounding: I couldn't fathom voluntarily walking directly to such a scary place.

I sat with five or six boys in an orderly circle in her back yard, right at the edge of the jungle. She told us something about bluebirds, successfully diverting me from terror involving a panther that I expected to jump me at any moment. The pictures helped, too.

Then it was refreshment time: a Dixie cup of cool water and a few crackers. Plain square saltines.

Now, this was great: I loved saltines, and still do. I forgot all about tigers and snakes, and cheerfully ate my couple of crackers and drank my cup of water. I began to relax a little. I decided that panthers probably don't eat people who are themselves eating crackers.

Afterwards we were supposed to run around and play. I was a little uncertain about running around in the jungle, but found something to amuse myself for a while, and then we went home.

Unfortunately for me, that was the summer's last meeting of The Bird Club, and next summer it did not resume. The Bird Club appears to have died out.

Funny how a few sentences and pictures about bluebirds, and a few saltines and a cup of cool water can convert the unfamiliar and terrifying into something pretty nice.

I'll certainly never understand it.

Birds and Bees and Flowers and Us

I was talking with my son in law recently about the colors of birds.

My gregarious wife and I were in the Texas hill country—near Austin—with him and our daughter, looking at wildflowers.

If you've never been there, the hill country is noted for wildflowers in all colors, ranging from the famous bluebonnets to tiny yellow things with witty pinpoint blossoms.

All this color and variety interested me. Now, my son in law is a very bright man, and an accomplished naturalist, who maintains careful lists of wild birds and flowers he has observed.

He likes our birds in western North Carolina, especially the lemon-colored finches that pop up around this time of year and crust our feeders like jewelry.

I mentioned that I wondered just why some birds needed to be so flamboyant. Why in general do birds and flowers have to be all that attractive? Wouldn't the adaptive uses of nature be satisfied with something less elaborate?

I suppose I had something like bar codes in mind.

Well, he said, of course we know that the colors serve for identification and discrimination: birds probably use them to recognize their own.

In many cases, he reminded me, color patterns, particularly in bugs and butterflies, seem to succeed because they outsmart predators. And the flowers have distinctive colors to advertise to the bees—they have inventories of pollen to move.

Paul Cox

But there's no way to demonstrate whether birds have any aesthetic sensibility that their markings satisfy. Or bees—maybe they do, but we don't know it.

So then, he said, why not? You could have drab markings that do the same trick, but what would be the advantage?

We came upon a hillside that looked to me like a Monet painting—a green slope splashed with long washes of purple, yellow, and pink, punctuated occasionally with deep crimson points. Huge blue skies with rich cotton clouds, and ancient oaks looking maternal and content.

As you might expect, tourists were lined up all along the roadside with their cameras taking this scene in, as we did. And you would have, too.

I read somewhere that humans, given a choice, tend to find landscapes loveliest that most resemble those where we lived and thrived during the longest stretches of our past.

It's as if something deep inside us responds to certain sights—and sounds and smells—because they work for us. Like birds and bees, we seem automatically to like those things that we need.

One analysis of this would be just that attraction to healthful things and revulsion at poisonous things simply serves the survival purposes of nature. Natural selection at its best.

But there's another way to say it.

It's spring, and we see around us a world that we find beautiful. We can divide that perception into two aspects: the world itself, and our response to it.

To put it simply, we can be thankful for living in a world to which we have adapted by simply smiling back when it smiles at us.

And, equally important, for having the gift of responding with pleasure—with aesthetic gratification—to certain colors, smells, and sounds. The joy itself is a blessing.

The gift for appreciating is as important as having something around us to appreciate. A blessing—and curse—of self-consciousness is to know when we are pleased.

By the way, my son in law is also an excellent photographer—he has a great eye for what needs to be looked at and appreciated, and works hard to get a shot just right.

I can appreciate that, too.

FOOD, SO TO SPEAK

Eggplant and Other Culinary Horrors

I have decided that there are three types of people who eat eggplant. None is completely healthy.

First, there are a few people who eat eggplant because they actually like it. There are, I think, fewer than 40 of these people, and most live on other continents. Far, far away from us.

Second, there are those who eat eggplant to mortify the flesh. They believe that suffering is redemptive, and eat eggplant precisely because they don't like it.

These are the spiritual descendents of emaciated eremites who flogged themselves in caves with briers and wore hair shirts until their bodies were raw and ulcerous.

I don't know how many such people there are: they don't have to check in with me.

But the largest group of eggplant eaters comprises people who want to be identified as the kind of people who eat eggplant.

Here's what I mean by that.

People like to swim against the current a little, to have personal distinctions. Eating eggplant can be such a distinction. If you are one of these people, you will eat some eggplant from time to time, and then next morning as soon as you get to the office you tell everyone you see: "I ate eggplant last night!"

Notice the audience's reactions. The eggplant eater thinks those are admiring glances.

Moreover, eggplant is an ancient and mysterious vegetable. It smacks of venerable foreign cultures; it exudes glamorous ethnicity. It is heavy and purple, a little shiny.

I have heard that there is some kind of Arabian proverb to the effect that a suitable bride must know a thousand ways to prepare eggplant. (I think this is despicable anti-Arab propaganda, but we were discussing eggplant.)

It's like the French eating snails. Now, nobody really likes snails, except maybe some birds, but people eat them so others will admire their openness to exotic cultures.

"Not eat zee snell? Ah, m'sieu: you have not zee cul*tu*re!"

Like that.

People with dark eyes and sultry secrets voluntarily eat eggplant. I want to be like such people. *Ergo.* . . . That's the reasoning.

Take liver. When I was young my mother—indeed, I think all adults—encouraged me to eat liver.

I tried it once, and found that it is just gristle embedded in lukewarm clay.

Nowadays people note that the liver is some kind of sludge trap for bodies, and it is therefore considered dangerous to eat.

But some people persist in eating it. I even saw a guy, who was being taken to lunch for his birthday, order liver in a restaurant.

We didn't make much of it, though, because we knew he was just showing off. He ate the liver not because he liked it, but because it was a feat to swallow it at all, and he was courting panache.

Same with eggplant.

My adventurous wife has a dish involving eggplant. You split this eggplant lengthwise, put on some tofu (yes, tofu) and soy sauce, and somehow roast the whole thing.

She likes to make this dish in the way a person likes making things with Lego's: what you make isn't important, but it's fun to make it.

The first bite of this dish is pretty good, I'll admit. Only problem is that a serving has thousands of bites in it, and they become increasingly distressing.

So she and I have reached an agreement concerning the use of eggplant in our home. We made a pact, to-wit:

Article 1: My wife won't prepare or serve eggplant.

Article 2: I won't blow the house up with dynamite.

I think that's a win-win resolution.

Broccoli and the Presidency: An Analysis

A few years ago President Bush—the Elder—became notorious for saying he didn't like broccoli.

He declared that he was the President of the United States, and as such he didn't have to eat broccoli if he didn't want to.

And he didn't, so he didn't.

I was alarmed, so I checked the US Constitution. Sure enough, there it is in Article XII: "No President of the United States may be compelled by legislation, legal precedent, culinary fiat, or medical directive to eat any food the aforesaid President dislikes or for any other reason prefers not to eat." Imagine that!

The basic problems with broccoli are these.

First, broccoli has a poor reputation. People think of it as icky, but it isn't. Not that icky.

Actually, it has been proven that if you blindfold a rat and feed it broccoli, it thinks it has eaten a cheeseburger six times out of ten. But I dislike thinking of rats, especially rats who have eaten a cheeseburger six times, so let's return to broccoli.

Second, people eat frozen broccoli, which seems to be made of plastic. That is: hard and tasteless, as I know because once when I was a child I ate part of a plastic rattle.

Do they make plastic toys out of frozen broccoli? Just asking.

Third, modern broccoli is too big. People find broccoli the size of box shrubs to be off-putting. It produces unhealthful mealtime stress.

Biting into such ungainly foods seems like starting a long, boring, difficult project. Where do you stick your fork? It is easier to eat peas, which come in more convenient packaging units.

Fourth, broccoli seems to be not one vegetable, but many. We need to analyze.

There are two general aspects to the broccoli manifestation. One is the trunk; the other is the bole.

The trunk of the broccoli, sometimes called the "stem," is the woody part. This is the part that fancy restaurants sell to non-fancy restaurants, and they in turn put into your salad.

This trunk is subdivided into two segments. First is the trunk proper, fabricated from wood, string, and other manufacturing material.

It is all right to eat this part, but you have to be an accomplished chewer, and patient. You might warm up with a few tent pegs.

Near the top, the trunk becomes several little sub-trunks. These are designed to resemble those big metal-and-concrete things they put into the water to damage the hulls of invading warships.

But they're a little more edible. Pretty much the same as the trunk proper, but slightly more entertaining, in case you're bored.

The bole of the broccoli is sometimes called the floret. I used to know a fellow named Irving who was sometimes called Ichabod. Same kind of thing.

Anyway, many people think broccoli boles are the best part. And they would be, except that when you bite them, they disintegrate into tiny pellets that hide in the crevasses between your teeth.

Finally, I find that if I write the word "broccoli" as many times as I have in this essay, it begins to look funny to me.

It reminds me of a family friend I haven't seen in years, who married a guy with a strange name. So then she had that strange name herself. Got to where I couldn't think of her as the same person, because she had such an odd name. We drifted apart.

I wonder whether that was part of President Bush's problem with broccoli. The Elder, I mean. I don't know how the Younger feels about it, although I suppose you could ask.

A Lesson Involving Peanut Butter

You can tell something about a person from observing what he or she does with peanut butter.

A few years ago, the main objective of a peanut-butter eater was to keep the goop from sticking to the roof of the mouth. You could dell wed dat happa becaud perdon cuddo dalk plade!

Now, though, they put so much slippery stuff into peanut butter that it can't stick to anything much except bread and maybe army blankets. This isn't a complaint, however, because it does taste better this way.

Years ago, I didn't fully appreciate the romance of peanut butter. I enjoyed it, and I snickered when the Girl Scouts returned from what they thought of as a camping trip raving about a dish they enjoyed. Seems they cored an apple and stuffed a mixture of peanut butter and raisins into it. Then they ate the whole thing.

They claimed this was really good, really fun, really all sorts of stuff, but I thought it was silly. This was no way to eat peanut butter or apples, and certainly an inappropriate camping activity.

I disregarded the whole matter. Their wild reports certainly never impacted my leguminous practices.

When I got old enough to realize there was more to the world than I had previously thought, I began to fear that maybe I didn't understand how to eat peanut butter correctly. I was intimidated by people who, I figured, must know stuff I didn't know, simply because they had lived places I had never been.

My puerile self-confidence was in crisis.

Paul Cox

I met people who assumed the standard way to eat peanut butter was with jelly. Usually grape, among us southerners, but strawberry elsewhere.

I was shocked—and then ridiculed for my own tastes! How could a previously friendly world have become so perverse?

But my introduction to horror was not yet complete. I subsequently learned that some people eat peanut better in even other ways. With cottage cheese. With bananas (not bad, actually). With lettuce, inexplicably.

The greatest outrage, I report with sorrow, came from my omnivorous wife. Get this now: peanut butter, strawberry jelly, salami, mustard, and onion. I learned of this after the wedding.

I must concentrate very hard on positives.

Nowadays, to make matters worse, she has a taste for eating peanut butter off a spoon. She walks around waving a big brown protein lollipop. I know this is wrong, but I keep my silence.

Anyway, here's the bad part. The people who make and devour such monstrosities with peanut butter seem pleased by what they've done.

And I, who use the food in the way I still consider correct, am ridiculed. But it isn't fair. I have as much right to my ways as anyone. So I am going to gather my courage and tell you my method.

It is this: peanut butter with mayonnaise on light bread. There. I've told you, and I honestly don't feel any better.

Confronting one's timidity is supposed to work better than this.

Here, anyway, is what I meant when I said you could tell something about a person from observing what he or she does with peanut butter: you can find out that some people are pretty weird.

I don't really know why you would want to find that out, though.

One other thought. When I got to be around forty, peanut butter began to disagree with me. I think it was I who changed, not the peanut butter.

Anyway, I don't eat it now. Never.

Life doesn't get any simpler, does it? Maybe that's what peanut butter teaches us.

Horrifying Peanut Butter Usages

My friends, we live in a world gone mad. I have the proof.

In a recent column I described some, um, interesting ways people have of combining peanut butter with other foods—and some near-foods. The climax of this was a description of my, um, interesting wife's favorite treat involving peanut butter, salami, lettuce, and strawberry jam.

Apparently she did this not in a bid to be spectacular, but because she thought it was tasty.

And it may be, for all I know. I certainly don't intend to authenticate the proposition.

I also expressed some diffidence about my own peanut butter history—it involved mayonnaise—which I had been intimidated into thinking somehow puerile and inappropriate.

Actually, I have always thought it's pretty good. But I developed an unfortunate digestive intolerance for peanut butter, and am therefore no longer in the game.

Anyhow, I've learned that peanut butter and mayonnaise is really tame and unremarkable. For I have now truly looked on the dark side of humanity and its peanut butter practices.

Upon publication of that column, I began to receive messages about peanut butter from readers. I was thinking of these as abject confessionals, but I began to realize they were offered as celebrations of inventiveness.

"Here's how I eat peanut butter," they implied, "And I'm proud to say so!"

In some instances these were people I thought I knew.

Len Arnold, for instance, described what he called a "fishing sandwich," because his wife won't let him eat it in the house.

I quote: "You start out with two slices of bread—I prefer cracked wheat—which you liberally smear with your favorite brand of PB. Add one large thick slice of sweet onion. Sprinkle with salt and a little pepper, and wrap securely. Refrigerate overnight."

The overnight refrigeration, he says, is the "real secret," because it allows the sandwich to "mellow" or "ripen" (or something). You go fishing with this sandwich and some beer. Sit at the downwind end of the boat.

You might not catch any fish, but you'll enjoy lunch.

Len, a Canadian, also tells me that the Canadian practice is not just to slap two pieces of bread—a PB piece and a jelly piece—together and eat.

No. Canadians, he says, mix PB and some jam together with a fork (he doesn't specify the kind of fork) in "a small custard cup" until the "colour" (whatever that is) looks good.

But, he acknowledges, Canadians talk funny, too. You bet your toque they do.

This was not the only such confession I received. I was appalled: celery, olives (yes, sir, olives), tomatoes, meats, and various cheeses got into the mixture.

A houseguest, whom I had thought harmless, described a Wisconsin practice of voluntarily ingesting peanut butter, any kind of cheese (so long as it's from Wisconsin, I suppose), and a piece of sweet pickle on a Ritz cracker.

If you don't have a Ritz cracker, you can substitute. One doesn't want to be punctilious, you know.

Another recent column described our cat's reaction to a bear who had happened into our backyard. When my wife held the cat up to the window to take a look, the terrified kitty immediately squirmed away and streaked directly under the bed.

She did not want to live in a world where she might see such things.

I'm thinking if I were to find a method for communicating with her all that I've learned about how people use peanut butter, she'd think the bear in the backyard a pretty manageable terror.

My gosh—all this in an election year!

A Gourmet's Guide to Fine Fast Dining

Americans like to eat fast food. This is not because we are energetic, busy people who should be admired. It is because fast food is easy, greasy, salty, and fattening; and we should be ashamed.

But we all sooner or later eat fast food anyway. We therefore need to give it a little thoughtful consideration.

It used to be that fast food meant a hamburger, or, if you had an extra dime, a cheeseburger. You routinely ordered this "all the way," which instructed the chef to sweep the condiment rack when garnishing your entrée. Onions were a little daring, but hey.

Nowadays, however, fast food means nearly anything: Chinese noodles cooked in a wok, pseudo-Mexican dishes, gyros, pizza, you name it.

Will you have options for garnish packages and beverages? Maybe, maybe not: that's a corporate marketing decision. Try to order a Coke in Pepsi territory, and you will be rebuffed.

It's not like Kiwanis or Rotary, American League or National League, Democrat or Republican, where you can make your own choice. Nope. The choice has often been made for you, and you get only to pay.

When there are decisions, they are baffling. Dipping sauce recipes are recited so swiftly that you can't follow. The query, "REEDGE ESKIP?" invites you to select between the "original" and the "extra-crispy" versions of a dish. Should you "super-size"? Should you take your lunch as a pre-defined "meal" or order a la carte? Do you want the chef to slop on some cheese-colored paste? What regional barbecue variant do you want?

And decisions about portion size are incomprehensible. A "small" beverage is huge; the "economy" size would keep a battalion in the tank all afternoon. "Double" may refer to the number of meat disks in your burger or to the number of discrete burger units (bun and all) in your meal.

You can take the options too far. I once had the bad luck to be behind a guy in MacDonalds who was trying to order medallions of veal in a marsala sauce. The child behind the counter thought he was cute, as he did. I did not.

You must coordinate your drink with your entrée correctly. Discriminating diners prefer a white beverage, such as 7-Up or Sprite, with chicken and fish sandwiches. With beef or other heavier meats, a dark beverage, such as Coke, Pepsi, or root beer, is indicated. Sweet tea with barbecue, of course.

Same with side dishes. Fries with a hamburger or with the fish sandwich. Chips with a chicken sandwich. Hushpuppies with barbecue. Pickle with a sub. Onion rings on special occasions with anything.

Beware of price inflation. Here's what I mean. You order a sandwich of some kind for an advertised price of $2.79, assuming three dollars will cover it. But when the maitre Mac'd announces your debt, it turns out to be well over $9. How did this happen?

Like this. The sandwich is in fact $2.79. The drink, a "small" 38-ouncer, is another $2.79. You casually mentioned fries, you idiot: another $1.37. Now add sales tax, shipping and handling, service fees, mustard tax, licensing fees and the county recording charge.

See how it happens?

Some fast-food places have salad bars. Sometimes these are OK, but other times they are just a few defeated and humiliated vegetables. You are expected to bathe these in a dressing that appears to be equal parts grease and Sakrete. There are midget tomatoes that look like red bubbles floating in white sludge.

These salad bars are designed to appeal to the health-conscious.

Makes you think, doesn't it?

The Cookie Issue

Believing, as I do, that people who address the public have a solemn obligation to confront important issues facing our society, I have decided to take up the subject of cookies.

Specifically, I intend to settle once and for all this question: what is the best cookie in the world?

I have conducted careful research. My investigations have taken me to many cities, in some of which I have eaten cookies. I have interviewed hundreds of people, generally about software, but that doesn't matter: I interviewed them. I have learned that best cookie in the world is the gingersnap.

A good gingersnap is hard, a little bitey to the teeth. It does not shatter upon biting, however: instead it comes off just in the shape of the teeth. It is a little gingery. For a fleeting instant you think it is going to be hot, but then it backs off and smiles in a rich sweetness that pleases but does not cloy. It is not filling: you can eat a gingersnap in passing without ruining your dinner.

When I was a teenager, my friends and I would take luncheon across the street from the high school at a concession stand in a tiny bus stop. There we would nourish our developing bodies with a Moon Pie and an RC Cola. We called this "a R-O-C and a Moom-Pie," because we were very cool, and back then that was the cool name for this dish.

A Moon Pie is a little complicated: soft yet, in a pliable way, crusty. Sweet, but with a nice leaven of dry cookie at its floor. Large enough to make an impression on the body, but not terribly filling. (The RC Cola, however, creates the illusion of satiety.)

I thought then that the Moon Pie was the best cookie on earth. If I had written this column back then, I would have said so. But in maturity, you see, we become wiser. Our tastes improve. I have come to understand cookies more clearly now, and now I see that the gingersnap is best.

I know that some readers will be fans of the macaroon, or even the Oreo. They may be distressed by what I have revealed, but I am prepared to defend my judgment.

Macaroons are indeed wonderful cookies. Part of the pleasure of a macaroon is that hours after eating it, you are still mining bits of coconut from between your teeth, and enjoying these as a private snack. This prolongs the joy of a macaroon, and argues powerfully for it. But many people are allergic to coconut. While this cookie might bring great satisfaction to those who love it, it is not edible by all. It must therefore not be estimated the finest cookie on earth.

I am sorry to say that Oreos, while tasty, are over-hyped. The contrived ritual of eating, where the cookie is dismantled and the innards devoured first, does not occur in nature. Only in TV commercials. And if I must destroy the cookie to eat it properly, then is not the design faulty? Think about this.

Further, when I bite a fresh Oreo, the top breaks apart, and I have to catch falling crumbs. This annoys me as much as the cookie itself pleases me. For safety, I must drench the whole confection in milk, which I then drip onto my shirt—more annoyance.

I would like to go on, but there is too much to say for one column. You are invited to confirm my findings on your own. Since your testing is for science, the calories don't count.

The Cookie Issue - Part II

Research into the question of the world's finest cookie continues. It is a public service that I am glad to perform. For you.

Now, let us establish to begin with that the best cookie available to humankind is the Fig Newton.

I don't know who invented it—probably somebody named Newton, come to think of it—but he or she was clearly a genius. The outer crust is just a little crumbly and chewy, and the inside distills the dark and sticky essence of many figs into one treat.

But the real genius of it is the little seeds. These are not hard enough to annoy, like the seeds of raspberries, but instead just crunch agreeably as you chew. They make a comfortable rattle in your mouth.

To eat a Fig Newton correctly, begin by biting off one corner. Then the next, leaving the bottom half of the cookie for last. You have the option whether to eat this in one pleasant bite, or to prolong the experience by eating it in two. Thus the brain is engaged as well as the tongue. Magnificent conception!

With that point settled, we need to discuss another kind of cookies that are now popular. These are the huge things that are sold from booths in malls. They look something like catchers' mitts.

There is, of course, nothing really *wrong* with such cookies. But are they really legitimate cookies? I find that if I should accidentally eat one during the day, I have compromised my enjoyment of dinner.

These things are more like sugar pot pies than true cookies. Just too big. Sorry.

The other cookie that needs to be dealt with is the snickerdoodle. This is a hard little bready cookie that children like to make.

And there you can see the problem. The snickerdoodle is a child's cookie. It has no particular character except that it is round and hard and sweet. And it is so easy to make that a child can make it.

I have found that adults who claim to favor snickerdoodles invariably adduce some happy childhood experience, usually involving a Brownie Scout activity, to back up their claim.

Of course, I appreciate pleasant childhood experiences, and eagerly support the Brownie Scouts. OK, yes ma'am: also the Girl Scouts and the Girl Guides and the Indian Guides and the Boy Scouts and the Cub Scouts and PONY League baseball and the South Avenue Bird Club. All that.

But we are talking about cookies here, a serious subject. We must not let ourselves be seduced into fruitless nostalgic rumination. Pleasure is fine, but our topic is cookies.

Now you take, by contrast, a good lemon square. A really good one has a very slight brittleness to the top, with a dusting of powdered sugar, under which waits a sunny sweet viscous mass of lemon paste. You have to pick it up by raising your whole arm, including your elbow, just keep it level. You don't want it to lose powdered sugar or become tragically deformed by gravity.

Think this is an easy cookie to make? Think a child could make a good lemon square? One that would satisfy a mature, world-class cookie judge? Harrumph.

Enthusiasts of other fine cookies, such as the anise drop and the little thin star-shaped Christmas sugar cookie, will, of course, find ways to disagree. And they may make a few valid points. But I stand by my decision: the Fig Newton is the best cookie on earth.

Of course, now, a good molasses cookie is pretty hard to beat, too.

Research will continue.

Cookie Research Project Continues

Researchers on the ongoing project to determine the world's finest cookie have announced new findings.

The finest cookie, we have learned, is the Christmas sugar cookie. This cookie, shaped variously like an evergreen tree, a star, a corpulent elf, or a reindeer, compensates unusual sweetness with unusual thinness, so that it never cloys.

It should be topped with either red or green decorative sugar. Some researchers believe the green sugar cookies are the best, but this finding is not definitive.

The report praised several virtues of sugar cookies.

First, sugar cookies are basically easy to make. Even youngsters can make them, if you don't mind some mess in the kitchen. But making sugar cookies is like playing the piano: there's no limit to how good you can get at it. Baking these cookies is therefore a rewarding lifetime avocation.

Second, it is now understood that the sugar cookie has neither calories nor cholesterol. Yes ma'am.

Third, sugar cookies are difficult to mail successfully. I once received a box of them in the mail from my grandmother, who was a better cook than distribution strategist. Of course, what I really got was a box of pleasant dust. Why is unfitness for mailing a benefit? Because in order to enjoy fine sugar cookies, the kind that are not commercially available, you have to go to someone's home. You have to pay a holiday visit. Once there you will have not only sugar cookies but a fine time, as well.

Paul Cox

The best sugar cookies demand skill from the consumer, on account of their extraordinary thinness. If you impetuously use your fist to grab a well-made sugar cookie, the product of a master baker (or mistress baker), you will be disappointed. You will clutch a handful of sweet crumbs.

No, you must lift the cookie delicately by its edges, and take small bites. The edgewise pickup is necessary because you don't want to rub the green sugar off the top of the cookie with a rough thumb. Small bites because your grandmother, who made the cookie, will be watching.

Contrast these cookies with the huge, unsubtle soft chocolate pones sold from little kiosks in malls. These cookies are like meatloaf sandwiches: big, chewy, and rich. They are popular, I know, because they deliver massive doses of sugar and chocolate. But they ruin your dinner and make you sluggish and grumpy. Research shows that sugar cookies make you alert and cheerful.

Now, the sugar cookie is not the only worthwhile confection available during the Christmas-Hanukkah-Kwanzaa season.

There is, for instance, that doughy little cookie that is shaped like a tiny hushpuppy, except that it's made with flour and sugar and little chunks of walnut and maybe some anise flavoring, and dusted with powdered sugar. A fine little cookie, to be sure, but not quite so fine as the sugar cookie, on account of the way the powdered sugar gets all over your jacket and tie and the nuts get in your teeth.

Moreover if you have the misfortune to hear something amusing while eating this cookie, you can inadvertently and impolitely laugh powdered sugar and nutmeats all over your neighbor's wife. I don't want to talk about this, however.

There is a little unsweet cookie made with sharp cheese and some kind of hot red powder that gives them a cunning little sting. Wonderful things, but after I eat a couple dozen of them, I find myself wondering why my mouth feels so tired.

Research will continue, of course. Until further information is available, readers are encouraged to begin at once practicing sugar cookie production. Readers' families will thank me.

The Corn Bread Rules

Break your bread; don't ever cut it. You pull off a single bite, butter it if you like, and eat the whole bite. That's what I was taught.

The idea was, as I read in a book, that tooth marks in a partially eaten piece of bread will disgust other diners. And the reason why you don't cut bread is that cutting compresses its surface and degrades its ability to sop up sauce.

Those are the nominal reasons. The real reasons are that those are just the rules. Period, no discussion.

Only problem is that there are other perfectly good ways.

We've all seen perfectly civilized people, when they are served bread in the form of a roll, begin their meal by carefully cutting the roll in half horizontally, and buttering each half. Then the bread is all buttered and ready when they reach for it.

It's a little ritual, like sweetening your tea, putting a napkin in your lap, and dressing your salad.

Is there something wrong with these people? Or maybe something wrong with the rules?

It's funny about rules. Most of them arise, I believe, from what were once good reasons.

Eventually the reasons disappear as times change, but the rules remain. Since we can't remember the original reasons, then we obey the rules just because they are rules. Makes no sense, really, but we do it.

I've noticed a shortage of rules for corn bread. But we like rules, so let's have some for corn bread. Why not?

Paul Cox

Maybe several sets of rules, since corn bread, like the people who enjoy it, can take many forms—as pones and muffins, baked in a pan, as hushpuppies, in sticks.

It seems to me that when eating corn pone (preferably with two parallel indentations where the cook's fingers mashed it), a bite at a time seems to work best. Same rule as for wheat bread.

And the method of cutting and buttering the whole thing like a dinner roll is appropriate for corn bread baked in a pan, or for muffins. So far, so good.

Hushpuppies you just pick up and eat. The only rule is to hurry, before somebody else gets most of them.

(Incidentally, I have observed that some people, when the hushpuppy is a larger, two-bite size, will take the first bite and then stare thoughtfully into the hushpuppy for a few moments. Watch and see for yourself. I don't know why people do that.)

Corn sticks require thought. One technique is to bite the top end off, and then, if you want to, butter the wound and take another bite. Repeat until you need another corn stick.

I recommend, however, a method from Pitt County, North Carolina, where I grew up. Usually we had on the table a little cruet of vinegar mixed with peppers, probably the best sauce on earth. What you do is bite the top off a corn stick, and then pour in a little of that vinegar, which soaks into the bread. It's good for what ails you.

Finally, there is a kind of delicacy that I have seen only in Tidewater Virginia. This is soaked bread—stale corn pone drenched in a bowl of pot liquor (the juice left over from cooking vegetables of any kind).

You eat soaked bread with a spoon, and it is surprisingly good. Here's a way that makes good sense, if you don't like pot liquor running down your arm.

OK: these are the corn bread rules. You know what to do.

In Defense of Fruitcake

A few years ago a comedian had a clever idea. He suggested that there were only really a few fruitcakes in the world, and that these were just circulated year after year as gifts. Nobody, the joke contended, ever actually ate fruitcake: we just give as gifts the same ones we got as gifts.

That joke became quite popular, and it continues to have some currency. But as a fruitcake partisan I take issue. There are some of us who actually like fruitcake, and somebody has to take a stand.

This unfortunate jest has damaged the popularity of fruitcake. So has the phrase "as nutty as a fruitcake." This gets shortened to the practice of simply calling the nutty person a fruitcake. And the reputation of the person and the cake thus suffers.

But here's what you can do.

Get your grandmother, or somebody's grandmother, to make a good fruitcake. It should contain candied fruits, of course: cherries, bits of orange, and stuff like that. Some nuts are good, especially walnuts and pecans. Some nice fresh almonds. Figs. Dates. A little brandy helps, if you don't mind it. Or you can use light rum. Not too much: this is not a machismo contest.

The batter should be rich, dark, and chewy, and the whole thing heavy. You eat fruitcake in small portions because large portions are hard to lift.

But here's the part that most people overlook. When you serve this fruitcake, lay it on its side on a plate and pour some heavy cream over it. If you want to sweeten the cream, that's OK, but not too much. The fruitcake is already sweet.

Of course you stored the fruitcake wrapped in a towel moistened with brandy. And of course you heated it before serving, but not enough to dry it out. You did those because fruitcake should be moist, chewy, and heavy. It should fill your entire head with flavors and textures suggesting Victorian opulence.

Don't smack your lips. You will want to, but it would be impolite, and fruitcake is a notably polite dish.

You want to eat it off a fancy little plate with a fancy little fork. Well, your hostess wants you to, and it's her fruitcake. That's the way to eat it in company.

But later, when you can't get to sleep, or when you have been following simple assembly instructions too long, you should get a chunk of fruitcake, lubricate it with the cream, and eat it off any old saucer with any old implement, or with none. Tastes great either way.

No matter how daintily you do it, you will get your fingers sticky. That's part of the fun. Just lick them off.

There are other ways to enjoy fruitcake, but I don't recommend them.

You can, for instance, go to a convenience store and buy things called fruitcakes, if you want to. But is this wise? Would you go to a convenience store for a fine watch? For a good quality wedding dress? No, of course not: you would go to a specialist.

Because the fruitcakes you get in these convenience stores are not to be eaten. These are the ones the joke is about: they are made as desperation gifts, like the Valentine's candy that comes in a heart-shaped box.

The point is that you can't cut corners with a good fruitcake. The whole dish argues for doing things a certain way, the right way, and getting rewarded for that diligence.

A fruitcake is more than dessert, see. It is a lesson in how to live. Try it.

Let's Hear It for—Corn!

My kids used to kid me (that's what they are for, I believe). They maintained that they had heard me say many times that my favorite food, in all its many forms, is corn.

Well, it's true. Think about it the next time you sit down to a nice long ear of sunshine-yellow corn on the cob. Put on a little butter—not too much—and just a little salt. Too much of either covers up the natural flavor. Now go methodically down the ear, about three rows at a time. Sounds as good as it tastes.

You can go around the cob, although I believe adults usually go across. It may not matter much in the long run.

My friend Larry invariably takes exactly two rows at a time. This is a point of pride with him: he leaves the neatest, cleanest corncob of anyone in the world. Then he beams with pleasure, and I am happy for him.

Think about corn bread, in all its many forms. Hushpuppies and plain corn pone are my favorites. They don't really need butter, but a little is sometimes nice. With barbecue (real eastern North Carolina barbecue, of course) you need corn sticks. With chili you ought to have corn bread of some kind, although I suppose eating crackers with chili can be tolerated.

And while you are thinking of corn dishes, don't forget grits. This is what intelligent people eat for breakfast, and they eat hominy for dinner, if they know what is good for them. And then popcorn for a TV snack.

The Maya and the Aztecs had special gods for corn. One was for the young corn, and I forget the other. The Maya described the stages in a child's growth by the number of tortillas he or she was given to eat per day.

I used to make a dish involving regular old corn niblets from a can and a few mild peppers. All you do is put these in a pan with a little salt and a little butter or margarine and move them around until you are tired of waiting. The corn should be a little meaty and firm by then, and ready to eat.

My wife doesn't like this dish, and you might not, either. She thinks meaty, firm corn isn't good, and uses words like "hard" and "dry" to describe it. But I like the dish, because it really tastes like corn.

I wonder how corn got its bad name. Why do people speak of foolish jokes as "corny"? The kind of banter that barbershop quartets pepper their shows with is considered to be "cornball" (but I enjoy it). People call other people whom they consider unsophisticated "cornpone."

Of course, distinctively American foods are often used as terms of gentle ridicule. We call clumsy or error-prone people "turkeys" and we call children "punkin" when we consider that they are being a little empty-headed. So I suppose it's natural that corn should be used in fun as well.

But it's hard to take a food seriously when its name also describes low humor. Imagine speaking of a "truffly joke" or a "veal en brochette skit." See what I mean?

But I suppose the real dignity of a dish depends on what you make of it, and of how good it is for you. If that's true, then there aren't many foods to compete with corn—in all its many forms.

Oh, I nearly forgot. There is also a form of corn that is used as a sauce for ice cubes. Gives them a good, hearty flavor, if you know what I mean.

Important Thoughts About Pizza

"No, no, no!" my mathematician friend exclaimed. "Pie are round! *Cake* are square."

He could have said "pizza" instead of "cake," and his point would have been the same—whatever it was.

Perhaps his point, aside from the fact that mathematicians are pretty funny people, is that some things ought to be done only in certain ways, and people take this very seriously.

So seriously that they quarrel over them. Should pizza be round, served in pie-shaped wedges? Should it be square, the way some chains sell it, cut in squares and rectangles? Is it OK to use a fork?

What should be on it? Is pineapple permissible? Tuna? Or is it improper to wander far from the standard canon of toppings, such as onions, pepperoni, sausage, black olives? Anchovies can be a fighting matter in some circles.

You've probably read about pizza preferences in cultures other than ours: the Japanese are reported to like fish on pizza, and Spaniards like octopus. And as I understand it, some people actually do like pineapple. Broccoli, even.

Of course, in our right minds we don't really worry about such things. As serious adults we worry only about important issues. Yeah, sure.

Have you ever heard of the Stormy Synod of Whitby? This was the sixth-century ecclesiastical conference that shaped the future of the English church for hundreds of years. One of the major topics debated was how monks should get their hair cut. Believe it or not, there were three competing styles, or "tonsures," on the table. I can't for the life of me recall which won.

Maybe because I don't really care. But the Whitby conferees did: careers and the ecclesiastical future of England were at stake.

As you can imagine, there was a larger political issue behind the issue of monastic tonsure: and it was settled by a political maneuver that I used to remember something about.

What does this have to do with pizza?

I think just this. When somebody tells you something is not important, that usually means that it's important. It is important to that person in a way he or she can't possibly explain, in a way that would appear to be nonsense to somebody else, but not to that person.

Now consider this.

One day a few years ago I was conversing with a woman in my office about food. Diane is a Black woman from Louisiana, and I am a White man who grew up in North Carolina.

We were reminiscing about southern foods, which were not always easy to get in Chicago. We talked about collard greens, country ham, corn bread, sweet potato pie, grits, red-eye gravy, and of course fried chicken.

A friend happened by, a fellow of Italian ancestry. He listened for a while, and then asked incredulously: "What on earth are you two talking about?"

"Why, food," we told him. "Just about plain old familiar natural food. Home-style food like we grew up with."

"Grits? Sweet potato pie? Collards? What, are you people crazy? I never heard of such stuff."

We were a little offended, of course. Was he speaking of our plain, simple, southern-American fare? What was his problem?

"Well, it's just strange. I can't imagine anybody eats like that," Frank said. "Why not ordinary American food instead of all that goofy stuff you're talking about?"

Then we saw the light. What kind of "ordinary American food?" we asked him.

"Oh, you know, just regular food. Ravioli. Lasagna. Spaghetti. Pizza. Tortellini. Stuff like that. Stuff everybody eats."

Makes you think, doesn't it? Maybe sometimes pie are square after all.

The Importance of Potatoes In Western Thought

Most people don't really know much about potatoes, such for instance as how to spell them. But enough of political humor.

There are essentially two kinds of potato: Arshtaters and Sweettaters.

Arshtaters are divided into several types, or clans. There's the Katahdim, the Idaho, the Russet, and the French fried. Also the curly fried, although they cost more because you have to harvest them by unscrewing them from the ground.

There are also the little fancy red ones that come with the roast beef. These seem really good, until your waiter refers to them as "your starch," and then they begin to taste a little like good quality library paste.

Nobody refers to turnips that way, but who likes turnips to start with?

Arshtaters came from Peru, originally, but that's not why we call them "Arsh." No, we call them that because they grow a lot of them in Arland, which is across the ocean somewhere.

And of course, you don't really raise potatoes. You punch their eyes into the dirt and then they grow underground. You have to shovel them up; it's like a treasure hunt. Is this any way to grow vegetables?

If you eat the eyes of potatoes, your vision does not improve. You will have some wonderful tales to tell, however, when you get older.

Paul Cox

You can explain to your grandchildren someday how you used to eat the eyes of potatoes, and they will reply, "Ew!"

That will be fun for all.

My discriminating wife's favorite species of potato is the mashed, or, if you prefer, the smashtater. She likes it with butter and garlic. Enough garlic to make your eyes sting.

Speaking of that, have you ever had that kind of garlicky potato salad that you get in a Spanish restaurant? This dish is so good it persuades me that Spain must be a nice place, although I personally have never been there.

I have, however, been to Montreal.

Anyway, that's about all there is to know about Arshtaters. Now we turn our attention to Sweettaters.

These come in two different kinds: regular and yam. There's no difference between those unless you are a botanist, and even then you don't really care.

It's like the differences among turtles, terrapins, and tortoises. Do you think you know which is which? See what I mean, then?

I used to know a fellow in Dixon, Mississippi, who claimed he could eat more yams at a sitting than anyone else in the world. But when I put his claim to a rigorous examination, his documentation proved suspiciously thin. I doubt he was telling me the truth. He was married to a girl named Dinah, who had reddish hair. (The reddish is an altogether different vegetable, though.)

I'm not sure I know exactly what "home fries" are supposed to be. I think they're big chunky fried potatoes, but what is "home" about them? In our home, we don't make them like that. Do others? I've asked several friends and acquaintances, and none has ever fixed home fries at home. So naturally, I'm suspicious.

People should investigate things that sound suspicious that way. If you don't, what happens when a UFO comes your way? Nobody would believe you, and what would be the point?

I seem to have wandered off the subject, and that's risky. I think we were speaking of a time when Vice-President Dan Quayle was dining in a Spanish restaurant. I don't really know anything about that, I'm afraid. Sorry. False alarm.

I can tell you, however, that Montreal gets really cold in the winter. Oh, boy!

The Decline And Fall Of Onion Rings

Well, actually, it's about the decline and fall of me, but I'd rather put it in terms of onion rings.

I've read that a person's life should have some aesthetic shape to it, like a good novel or a Beethoven symphony. The parts fit together in a satisfying way, they have a pattern, they make sense.

And lately I've been thinking about this in terms of onion rings.

When I was young and at the height of my powers (ahem), some friends took me to a drive-in place one evening for onion rings.

A drive-in place, for those of you who are young and at the height of your powers, was a place where you drove up and parked your car in a nice row. A teenager came to your car, took your order, and then brought it to you. You never had to leave the car.

Why was this good? Who knows, but it seemed very cool at the time, so of course we went. Part of the entertainment often was teasing the "car-hop," as I recall, but it was good-natured and in fun. We teased and then we tipped, so everything evened out.

Anyway, my friends went to this drive-in, with me in the car, and ordered onion rings—a dish I had somehow never before tasted.

These were remarkable onion rings. There were big, juicy, richly flavored loops of onion with a salty, slightly greasy batter extravagantly applied. The rings were hot, crisp (the odious word "crispy" hadn't been coined yet, so these were just good old crisp), and priced at about a quarter for a huge pile.

Needless to say, my life at that moment assumed a new purpose. I was a changed man—an onion-ring eater! I was devoted to onion rings.

But coincidentally, that evening I hit the mountaintop of my onion-ring-consuming career. Just like that: the first taste was the ultimate taste.

See, there's a certain tragedy implicit in this. Note the aesthetic implications: now follow the arc of the career.

Shortly after that, the drive-in place closed. Forever.

But my hunger for onion rings was forever un-slaked. Everywhere I went I ordered onion rings, hoping to recover some of that first ecstatic etc etc etc. You've read such stuff before.

But, as you might expect, I never was able to recreate that first perfect rapture.

Other onion rings were too heavily breaded. Flat tasting. Stringy little apologetic wisps of onion buried in gummy, doughy casings. Cold. Fried in fish grease. Stuck together. Sour batter.

They gave me indigestion, a headache, and a mournful heart. But I soldiered on, ordering onion rings, enjoying sometimes a flicker of goodness that served only to remind me—cruelly—of a glorious moment irretrievably lost.

You see where the arc of this story leads, I suspect.

Lately I have suffered what I believe is the final blow in my quest to recover my primal onion ring joy: I have learned that onion rings are bad for my health.

They are too salty, too greasy, too something or other else, probably. I have been compelled by dietary prudence to renounce onion rings—until, like the drive-in place, I, too, go out of business forever.

Pizza will probably be next, and then I'll have a truly tragic song to sing. And if barbecue goes, I'm hope I'm out of here.

I suppose it's not the decline and fall of the Roman Empire or anything, but I hope you feel the poignancy of this little history.

Life, as someone has said, is a casting off. Lovely and touching, ain't it?

Ordering A Hamburger

"A hamburger, please."
"Fries?"
"No, just a hamburger."
"Plate?"
"Well, yes. I mean, it comes on a plate, doesn't it?"
"You get fries or chips with the plate. You want chips, then?"
"No, just a hamburger."
"What with it?"
"Nothing. A hamburger."
"What kind of cheese? We have American or Swiss."
"Not a cheeseburger. A hamburger."
"I can have them take the cheese off. That's 50¢ extra, though. You want that?"
"Why should I pay extra not to get something? Look. All I want is a hamburger. No chips. No fries. No cheese. No pickle. No pie. No little piece of parsley. No frangipani or souvenir turtle or lawn-care contract. Just a plain hamburger. And mustard, of course."
"You want the mustard-burger, then?"
"Mustard-burger?"
"That comes with applesauce and an onion ring."
"Is it not possible for me to pay you enough money to bring me the following: one hamburger patty in a bread disk, and a bottle of yellow mustard?"
"Well, see, it doesn't come that way. I can give you the Merri-Meel without garni. You get a drink with that."

"Merri-Meel? Garni? What are you talking about? The word for it is 'hamburger.' How is this hard?"

"Sir, I'm just trying to take your order. If you don't want the Merri-Meel, maybe we could dress down a Busy-Guy. That would be a hot dog, but we would substitute a patty-stack, and dress down means we only give you fries, and we could leave those off and give you a credit on the drink instead. What size drink?"

"I don't want a drink. Is a Busy-body a plain hamburger?"

"Well, normally a hot-dog, but we do what we call a twist on it, we substitute a patty-stack, and that's, yes sir, just a plain hamburger, with lettuce, tomato, pickle, and Silli-Sauce. That's like barbecue sauce?"

"I have departed the earth. Completely left the real world. I am quickly getting very old."

"Sir, I can see you're upset. Let me let you speak with the manager. Would you like that?"

"Does the manager sell hamburgers?"

"Hello, sir. I'm Todd? The day manager? How can I help you?"

"By selling me a hamburger. A plain hamburger, and allowing me to wring yellow mustard onto it from a plastic jar. Can you do that?"

"Well, see, sir, we like to make things nice for our customers? Like a little extra special? Customers seem to like that, most of them? So Trisha was just trying to help you decide on what you want to order?"

"Yes, and of course I think Trisha is a perfectly nice young woman. I appreciate her skills and diligence. Perhaps I'm being irascible, but really, all I want is a hamburger. I'm odd like that: I just want a plain hamburger."

"Well, sir, I agree with you one hundred percent? Trisha has been with us over four weeks now, great worker! But let's get right to your order. You say you want a Plain John without?"

"A Plain John without?"

"That would be a grilled patty on a non-sesame bun without nibble."

"Nibble?

"Chips, fries—something like that for your other hand."

"OK. OK. Bring me that, a Plain Jane or John Doe or whatever you called it. Without. A one-handed John Henry, if you will. And a bottle of mustard, if you have one."

"Well, sir, I'm afraid you're a couple of weeks late? We discontinued the Plain John? Other customers just really didn't opt for it in market-worthy numbers."

A long pause.

"I see. Hm. Do you, then, have something in a nice pistol? With?"

The Marmalade Question

I looked for some marmalade this morning, and couldn't find any. That got me thinking.

My raspberry-oriented wife asked why I was pawing through the pantry at break of day. I explained why, and she was bewildered.

"Well, there's plenty of perfectly good raspberry jelly right there in the refrigerator," she reminded me. "Eat that." I don't think she particularly likes me rummaging through the pantry.

And I can understand her feelings. I don't like her rummaging in my sock drawer, either, because she usually asks me why I don't throw away something to which I have inexplicable sentimental attachments. Socks that have been loyal to me over the years, you know. But we were speaking of marmalade.

The wife and I have had the raspberry conversation several times, and probably will have it several more.

The trouble with raspberries is symbolized by the absurd spelling of the word, with that perfectly useless "p" in the middle of it. It is there simply to get into our orthographic teeth, if you will permit me such a metaphor.

What I am trying to say in a clever way is that the seeds in raspberry jam stick between my teeth and worry the heck out of me. There.

The flavor is OK, but the seeds ruin the total experience. My father was the same way about spinach: said it got into his teeth. Not something you can argue about—successfully. He just smiled and said he couldn't eat spinach, and didn't.

Our raspberry conversation always bogs down when my wife brings up popcorn, which I like partly because it gets into my teeth. And figs, which I like but which also have tiny seeds. But those are different, I remind her, although I can't quite put my finger on how.

Anyway, she also reminded me of the many little colorful jars in the refrigerator: jalapeno-mint jelly. Pear butter. Garlic preserves. Stuff like that. All about half full (or half empty if you're a pessimist). Some dating back to the days when I last wore some of those socks.

You see, the truth is that I like from time to time I like to get off-beat kinds of jelly and jam just to see what they're like. They are all interesting and good, but not the kind of thing you want to spend the rest of your life with.

I even like a little Marmite on my toast sometimes. A word of caution, if you haven't tried Marmite: a little is enough. It's oddly enjoyable, if formidable. But we were speaking of marmalade.

Now, what I like in the morning is a nice bitter, rough-cut marmalade. Something that fights back a little, something with some backbone.

Something with some rind in it that I can chew on, and some tartness to quarrel with. A little toughness, a little spunk.

That's why I don't like my wife's second favorite toast decoration, strawberry jam. It's not bad, understand, but it's just sweet. Too easy. What's the point?

Anyway, to make a long story short (too late!), there was no marmalade. I did the only thing I could do: ate my toast plain and acted grumpy.

That was a pretty good substitute, I think. Set me up for the day just fine.

Her too.

You have to know how these things work. What gets into your teeth the right way, and what is just annoying about it. What works in the morning. How to handle these delicate early-morning searches for emotional equanimity.

Why don't they teach you this stuff in school? Instead of geography, maybe?

How To Make Fine Pudding

Making fine pudding isn't hard. You just have to know how to do it. I am referring to banana pudding, of course.

First you boil some water. I'm not completely certain why, but I think that in general, it is good to start a cooking exercise by boiling water. So boil some and stop asking me all these questions.

This is important to remember in the kitchen: asking a lot of questions will make the cook impatient. So don't do it. Boil water instead.

I'm not certain why cooks don't like to answer questions. Perhaps it's because they're busy, or concentrating on cooking. Best leave it alone and get back to the pudding.

Now, get you some bananas, and cut them up. You didn't cut them up small enough, so cut them some more. This is one of the first things I learned.

It has to do with the shape and dimensions of the pudding bowls, but you wouldn't know that automatically. If you bungle this part of it, though, then everyone will have to eat from the cooking dish, and that is unsanitary. Aren't you glad I'm here to help you?

Oh: peel them first.

OK, now check the water. Is it boiling?

Next you get sugar and some other stuff, and put it all into a big bowl. Look it over pretty carefully: is everything there?

This reminds me of a story about a man in Model, Alabama, who accidentally dropped his false teeth into a batch of Brunswick stew he was making. If you run into people from Model, ask them about this man, whose name, I believe, is Lester or maybe Rodney.

The water should be about ready now.

Did I mention that you would need some pudding mix? You get this from the grocery store, or you ask your wife to get you some from the grocery store. She will know which shelf.

This is the difference between men and women, incidentally: women intuitively know which shelf in the grocery store things are on. Men prefer to work it out intellectually.

Anyway, assuming you have this pudding mix, follow the directions on the box. You may want to make several boxes. In that case, follow the directions on each box, but multiply by the number of boxes. You will need a pencil.

And it's best not to write your figuring on the counter-top. Same reason as not asking the cook questions: just don't.

Now pour the boiling water into a bowl. Set this bowl aside where the cat can't get it. It is too hot for her.

Put the bananas in with the other stuff. Put some vanilla wafers in with the bananas. I forgot to mention those before, but ask your wife whether you have any. She will have remembered to pick some up, and you better not have eaten them yesterday afternoon. Same reason as before.

OK: now we have the bananas, the cookies, and the other stuff in a big bowl, and we have some boiled water cooling someplace where the cat can't find it. We have some pudding mix someplace. Find that.

Put everything all together. Mix until your arm begins to get sore. Put everything in the oven.

Come back after half an hour or so and turn the oven on. This is called "post-heating," ha-ha. Turn off the burner you boiled the water on.

When you are ready to eat this pudding, scoop it generously into big bowls. Assemble your family, who will swiftly eat it with big grins. Your wife will clean up, I'm sure.

See there? Easy!

A Few Words about Breakfast

Most people will tell you that breakfast is their favorite meal.

We Americans have a pretty settled idea what breakfast is. You can identify it at any popular hotel most mornings by looking at the breakfast buffet.

Eggs (usually scrambled), bacon, grits if you live in an enlightened area, fried potatoes, fruit juices, melon slices. Usually dry cereals with boxes of milk. Pancakes. Toast, muffins, doughnuts, bagels (usually bad). Oatmeal.

Coffee, of course. Unless, like me, you can't tolerate it. I take strong black brewed tea, or else nothing. No tea bags, please.

At fancier buffets, there is a person who cooks the eggs for you on the spot. This person is usually backed up, though, so you have to wait.

Extra dishes on the standard approved breakfast list might include biscuits and gravy, corned-beef hash, chipped beef over toast, and ham. Waffles. Omelets, eggs benedict.

Oddly, you never see anything outside a limited set of dishes for breakfast. When is the last time you saw fried chicken on a breakfast buffet? How about tuna casserole? Vegetable soup?

And the problem is that many of the standard breakfast dishes are now considered unhealthful. Eggs? Too much cholesterol. Bacon? Sodium and saturated fat. Coffee? Gives you the heebie-jeebies.

So millions of health-conscious Americans face an early-morning dilemma. And who wants to deal with a dilemma early in the morning—for no pay?

We usually solve the dilemma by eating some kind of "natural" cereal with watery skim milk. This generally makes us grumpy, so we can be better managers.

College kids eat cold pizza for breakfast. They are desperate.

Of course, people in other parts of the world have their own breakfast customs.

People in England eat what they call "rashers" of bacon. I used to wonder what a rasher was, until I learned it was just a serving. But perhaps calling it a "rasher" has a bracing effect.

And they eat "kippers." A kipper is a kind of canvas bag that you carry books in, I think. I could be wrong about that.

My genial wife and I once took a brief trip to Iceland, where breakfast consisted of a baloney sandwich hold the mustard hold the lettuce. It was awful. Iceland is a pretty place, but they have no idea what to do in the kitchen until at least mid-morning.

Here's how to have a great breakfast, regardless of what you eat.

First, breakfast is best early on a bitterly cold morning. This is important, and it makes me wonder why the Icelanders squander their obvious natural advantage.

Second, a memorable breakfast is sociable. Nobody eats a good breakfast alone. I don't care what you talk about, or even if you read the paper. It is important that somebody else be there.

Third, you should have something remarkable and interesting to do after breakfast. Maybe an important physical task. Maybe a trip. Maybe decorating the house for Christmas. Point is, if breakfast is to be grand, you should have the sense of stoking yourself for something.

Finally, everybody should share the work. If the wife does all the cooking and serving, some of the eating, and all the cleaning up, then nothing great happens. Everybody should participate, have a good time, and feel part of the event.

You won't have more than one or two excellent breakfasts a year. So go ahead: have an egg. A few a year isn't going to kill you, and it could make your life better, if not longer.

What To Do With A Basket of Crabs

Felix came early several mornings a week with fresh produce and genial conversation. My grandmother would say: "What's good this morning, Felix?"

"Got some peas, some real good butterbeans. Tomatoes good today. Corn. Got some nice okra here, but I won't have it long."

She always took an armful of vegetables, overpaid, and asked after Felix's wife.

Next came a job in which I participated. My grandmother put loose tea into a strainer, and that into a huge glass jar of water, which she sealed.

My job, then, was to carry this out to some corner of the porch where it would get plenty of sun. Later in the afternoon my job would be to bring it in again.

Some days my brother and I would then go crabbing. Crabbing—as we did it—involved many thrilling adventures, not the least of which was accidentally spilling a basket of crabs onto a neighbor's lawn where adults, children, and several excitable dogs were being sociable. Talk about a scramble! But that's not today's topic.

We got home with the crabs and my grandmother sighed: "What am I going to do with all these crabs?"

Well, she was just being silly, I knew, because I realized that she understood perfectly what to do with a basket of outraged crabs.

That's because she was a woman, and, as I understood the world back then, women knew how to turn things into meals. They understood cooking. I did not, and it didn't dawn on me that males could understand such things.

I wasn't worried about what she would do.

Anyway, this happened when it was about time for me to bring the tea inside: brown and warm as a sleeping cat. I brought it into the house and set on a corner of the kitchen counter, out of the way.

My grandmother dumped the furious crabs into a big pot of cold water and turned on the stove. This was in tidewater Virginia, not Maryland, so she didn't use strong seasonings. We liked a delicate flavor to our crabs; and we persuaded ourselves that they didn't mind being boiled.

She made what my brother and I called "jelly," but what was actually just plain old Jell-o. It came in three flavors, red, green, or yellow.

Oh, you think those are colors? Nope, they're flavors, as you would know if you had ever eaten Jell-o.

My grandmother made Parker House rolls. That is, she created a slippery dough by some means I don't understand, and then, as she stuck the rolls into the indented pan, she gripped each one quickly in a certain way, so they had a little doughy fold at the top when they came out.

She united some corn and Felix's little lima beans into a cheerful bowl of mellow succotash.

When it all was ready, my grandmother spread a cloth on a table on the back porch. I thought it was pretty elegant at the time, but that's because the cloth covered up the paint drippings. And the chairs didn't exactly match, but that didn't appear to be an issue.

My grandfather, a quiet, genial man, came home with a little whistle, and we all sat on the back porch near the pecan trees and had supper: a pyramid of steamed crabs, hot fresh rolls with butter, dramatic rounds of thick red tomatoes, iced tea with fresh mint leaves from the yard, succotash, and then Jell-o for dessert.

And quiet, pleasant conversation. No boisterous kid talk, no quarreling.

Did I mention that my grandfather always came home with a genial little whistle?

MEMORIES

Digging Holes

I told my crafty wife, "I'm going downstairs to write a column about digging holes."

"Speaking of digging holes," she replied, "When are you going to dig some holes so we can transplant the...."

And I realized that I had just dug myself into yet another one.

When I was a kid, digging holes seemed like fun. It must be grand to step down on a shovel, come up with a nice bunch of dirt, lay it aside, and do it again.

Pretty soon you would have a nice pile of dirt over here and a nice hole over there, both great to play in. And the digging itself would be fun.

Our grandfather said he was having fun when he turned up his garden every spring, shoveling out a wedge of dirt and putting it into the hole from which he had taken the previous wedge. Punching it with the shovel to loosen it up, and then blading out a new one.

He could go through the whole garden plot like that in an hour. Then he would drink iced tea on the back porch.

One morning my cousin Lemuel, who lived next door, dug a stump out of his backyard. My brother and I had several questions for Lemuel, but as the morning progressed his replies became less forthcoming.

He dug a splendid hole, though. Had to stop every so often and chop through roots, and he sweated quite a bit, but I was sure he was having great fun.

Then he pulled the stump out with a rope, and chopped it up. Even more fun.

So my brother and I decided to dig us a hole. We didn't have a stump to justify it with, so we just decided, as many kids do, to dig until we got to China, where we would stop.

Probably at that very moment some Chinese kids were starting a nice hole all the way to America, where they too would stop.

We got our grandfather's shovel. It was, of course, grandfather-size, not kid-size. That meant it was at least twice as tall as I was. We didn't worry about that.

My brother stuck the blade of the shovel into the ground, where it immediately stopped. We realized he needed to step on it, so he did.

He rose about a foot off the ground, teetered, and fell off as the shovel came down and hit him in the head.

It wasn't supposed to do that.

Well, we struggled for what seemed like a good while—probably about fifteen minutes, of course—and managed to get our hole maybe four inches deep. And about as big around as a peanut butter jar.

This was a good beginning. We took turns squatting down and putting our eyes to the hole, to see whether we could identify any Chinese people down there. I couldn't, but my brother said he could. He was older, so his eyes were stronger.

Now it was time to sit on the back porch and drink iced tea. We explained this to our grandmother, because we didn't know how to fix iced tea.

She demanded the right to inspect the hole. "You didn't dig up my irises, did you?" We didn't really know, but doubted we had done that. And lucky for us, we hadn't.

We showed her the hole, and explained that when we finished, we would take her on a trip to China with us.

I think she was pleased. We certainly were, and we all had a nice glass of iced tea.

There.

Now as to this transplanting thing. Maybe I should start another column. Something about resting.

How I Spent My Summer Vacation

Around forty years ago I was accidentally offered a plum summer job driving a laundry truck. The pay was good, for then, and the work seemed easy and fun.

I was to drive around a village in hilly northwest Georgia, picking up dirty laundry and dropping off clean.

The incumbent was retiring after some forty years. He was to train me for a week, and then take his station on his front porch. Sounded good to me. I jumped at it.

Because I was entirely clueless.

First day he said it was easy. Cluelessly, I thought that meant it was easy.

We drove along winding roads, not all paved. We stopped at various houses, picking up a bundle, dropping off a bundle. Some houses belonged to the opposition laundry, so we didn't pick up their bundles. Easy work. Pleasant.

"This here's Acorn Road. It ain't on the map, so you got to remember it. We'll go part way down and then swing over to Daniels'."

"Daniels Road?" I asked, studying a map.

"Well, no. Ain't no Daniels Road around here. Going to Ben Daniels', pick up some laundry. We have to pick up there on Thursday, too, but at his daughter's house. Deliver around back. Then we'll swing over to Sowers Road."

"Sore's Road?" I asked, trying to find it on the map.

"Sowers Road," he replied. Sounded all the same to me, but he didn't offer any spelling.

It was like that all week. No road signs, no landmarks except trees and billboards. No apparent order to the route.

At first I was in a quandary: do I try to follow the map, which was only vaguely accurate, or just pay close attention and try to memorize landmarks? Soon I gave up and just enjoyed the ride.

The routes crossed and overlapped, and some houses were on more than one route, like Ben Daniels'—only, one of those was his daughter's.

By Friday my head was a jumble of country roads, front porches, special instructions, bundles of dirty clothes warming in the sun.

On Friday the retiree wished me luck and unsentimentally went home to his rest.

Next Monday I loaded my panel truck with warm bundles of clean laundry and set off. Seemed as if I needed to head out this way and take the second left. I hoped inspiration or memory or something would come along.

Nope.

I spent a week cruising northwest Georgia. I began leaving bundles at random, and picking up any soft-looking parcel I saw on any porch, becoming progressively depressed.

After that first week I was assigned an assistant, a recent school dropout who appeared to hold a grudge against me.

He didn't help. All week we cruised about, quarreling, looking for clues as to our whereabouts. We nearly came to blows most days.

At the end of the second week we had dotted the entire area with other people's laundry, left sheetfuls of dirty clothes baking on customer's front porches, and never once, so far as I know, driven down the same road twice in the same direction.

When I resigned that Friday afternoon I don't think my boss was particularly upset. I'm putting it gently.

I see now that the only map of that route existed in the mind of the old gentleman who had dedicated his life to creating it in all its rococo complexity and hidden efficiency. When he retired, he took it with him.

We can succeed as adults in this life only if we learn to map our world quickly and accurately.

Summer school can be tough.

Summer School The Right Way

My friend Eddie had a big garden in his backyard. Our job was to irrigate it.

Eddie's father, a schoolteacher, was teaching summer school, so he asked Eddie and me to keep his garden watered.

So we did. For a day or two this consisted of our standing around, one holding the hose, and squirting water on the vegetables. Not much fun.

But then Eddie's father made a little suggestion for an irrigation system. Since the garden was planted in rows, there were natural channels between the rows.

If we could figure out how to get the water to flow down those channels, we could just leave the hose on trickle for an hour or two every day, and that would get the job done.

Hm.

So we tried it. We took a hoe and cut a channel across the top of the garden, perpendicular to the rows. Turned on the water.

Not a good result. Almost all the water flowed into the first two rows, and almost nothing to the other end of the garden.

We tried putting the hose in the middle of the garden instead of at one end, but that didn't work either: the farther out rows didn't get any water. We had to work on the design.

So we put our heads together. We reasoned out that we should set up a system so that the initial flow from the hose ran into a channel which split in two. Then each of those themselves split in two, and each in two again.

This should assure an even flow among eight rows of vegetables. But then we counted the rows: nine.

So we worked some more, and figured out how we could make an initial split into three sub-channels, by adjusting the width and depth of the channels and setting smaller channels uphill from larger ones.

Now, this wisdom didn't come easy. We spent many days in Eddie's backyard, digging little ditches and making dams, testing with the hose, and hollering.

Part of the fun was that occasionally the wall of one of our little ditches would crumble, and water would spill over into another ditch. When that happened, one of us would holler: "There's a leak!"

And the other, of course, hollered back: "Well, dam it!" We always made a point to say this a little louder than we really had to. We were pretty good spellers.

Finally, we had figured out a system that worked. It took us a good part of the summer, but we got it. We could just turn on the water, and the flow from the hose would course evenly past each plant. Just right. We felt pretty good.

Eddie's father seemed impressed. "You boys have done a really good job," he said. "Very good work. Only problem is, now, that not all the vegetables need the same amount of water. Tomatoes and okra need the most. Peas not so much. Collards about the same as peas." He went on to explain which needed the most.

Of course, we weren't completely clear just which plant was which, so we needed a little botanical coaching to get the point.

So we went back to the design board. A couple more weeks of ditching and damming, and once again we had it.

At the end of the growing season, Eddie's family had a great garden, and we had had a terrific summer.

Neither of us grew up to be hydraulic engineers, of course. We didn't know we were supposed to be learning stuff.

Some people, you know, are just naturally gifted teachers.

A Good, Long Conversation

The best conversations, I've found, last a long time. The really good ones continue for years.

I've been pretty lucky with long conversations.

My mother and I pursued an ongoing talk about religion for many years. We disagreed about nearly every part of this subject.

That was all right. Differences of opinion are an important part of a good conversation. In fact, much of what I learned in that conversation was that there's nothing wrong with honest disagreement. I learned to respect it.

When I was a kid, I had a friend named Jimmy.

Well, who didn't? But he wasn't a fictitious person invented to make a point. My friend Jimmy was perfectly real.

He was a year older than me, but had been held back in school one year, so we were classmates. He had been held back because he had trouble with reading.

Everyone agreed that Jimmy was a smart fellow, and he really was. But he was dyslexic—his brain didn't process visual information in a way that made reading come easily for him.

Back in those days people whispered that he was "left-eyed" as if they were ashamed on his behalf. As for Jimmy himself, he didn't appear ashamed of anything.

He and I played together a lot, and we chattered the whole time. What Jimmy lacked in reading ability he made up as a talker. He always had something interesting to say.

I often disagreed with him, and always found that I had to think my views through pretty well to be able to stand my ground.

Jimmy and I talked about everything. Education. Girls. Religion. War—an interesting subject in the late 40's and 50's. Race—another interesting subject for small-town southern boys in those days. Parents—Jimmy was adopted, so he had a different slant that I found illuminating. Cars. Other kids. Everything.

While we talked, we did stuff. Plinked bottles with air rifles. Snuck off and smoked old dried-out cigars one of us had probably swiped. Fought elaborate, epic battles.

Some silly things, some dangerous things, some harmless things—kid stuff in the best sense. And we talked constantly.

I no longer remember many details, but I still hear those conversations. They resonate not in my head but through my whole personality. Jimmy and I helped build each other.

Our last substantial conversation turned on a pickup truck. He had an old one he wanted to sell when I was preparing to go off to college. I figured the truck would be the ideal way to take my stuff, and then I'd have transportation when I needed it.

But he refused to sell: said I would look like a dumb farmer driving a pickup truck on a big university campus. I was annoyed, but I knew he was thinking about what was best for me—even though once again we disagreed.

I lost touch with Jimmy as we grew older and took up different lives. I learned a few years ago that he had recently died of cancer, fairly suddenly and unfairly young.

Not having seen Jimmy for many years, I can't honestly tell you that I'll miss him.

One reason for that is that his company is available to me now as much as it has been for a long time, because, knowing him as well as I did, I've continued talking things over with him in my head all along.

No, I'm not hallucinating. Just revisiting, remembering things that might someday have happened. I find those imaginary talks satisfying and helpful.

The very best conversations, you see, never really end.

My Brief and Undistinguished Dancing Career

I saw something this weekend that brought back memories.

It was a clogging exhibition at an arts and crafts festival. In the exhibition young girls stood in lines and kicked around in time to spunky music. They seemed to be doing it reasonably well, and the spectators applauded heartily.

I've never been able to do that. The realization of my ineptitude at dance dawned on me gradually through my youth.

Younger readers: yes, we had dancing back then. My generation gave birth to rock n roll, in fact. Chew on that awhile.

But I was saying.

When I was ten or twelve or so, the local Girl Scouts used to have dances. If you were invited, you had to go, for reasons I never understood. I dutifully went and shuffled with all the other prepubescents, holding dreaded girls at arm's length.

A key moment came at one of those dances when a popular girl with whom I was exchanging torture on the dance floor finally remarked that my dancing was kind of unexciting. I was stung, and said, "I'm the one leading, right?"

She agreed, and I said: "So follow me."

I led her off the floor to the punchbowl and never asked her to dance again. One of youth's few painless memories.

Later, when I was in Raleigh for a statewide musical function, the organizers decided to entertain the participants by having a dance. One of the hostesses, noting me idle, insisted I dance. It seemed that everyone had to dance in order for her entertainment attempt to succeed. I was tender about her feelings, of course, but I didn't dance.

And as we discussed this absurd point, a realization flashed on me: dancing is really complicated. Not just the steps, but the whole idea of it. It means things to people.

Most people. Not me.

I think I lack an important gene or something. I can't seem to coordinate myself to music. I get dangerously clumsy and frighteningly fatigued. My mind seizes up. My knees lock. My feet feel distant. My arms flail like a left-handed bagpiper's (gosh, I don't know, but it sounds clever).

I just don't really feel what others feel when they dance.

Clearly people love dancing. There is pleasant physical movement, and a combination of "I-feel-good" along with "look-at-me" about it that I can see an argument for. In the abstract. But I can't do it.

My lack of dancing constitutes one of my dedicated wife's major life sorrows. She wants to dance, loves to dance, but dances alone. Dances around the house. Sways and places her feet with untaught art to any music. Well, not so much to Gregorian chant, but you know what I mean. She has her CDs and I have mine.

For awhile, I tried to be a good partner. I did attempt to dance with her the night we got engaged. I was, I'll admit, under the influence of the, um, music. But alas, I was clumsy and useless. That evening effectively ended my dancing career for good.

Some philosophers of aesthetics have argued that dance is the essential human expressive activity. You can understand all we do, beyond meeting our basic needs, as a form of dance. Conversation, etiquette, sports—all the little movements and gestures of civilized human interplay derive from the same impulse as dance, they argue.

And there is sense to that, I believe. Like love and music and play, dancing lets us be truly human.

Some of us, that is. Me, I dance about as successfully as a mailbox post. And there appears to be no cure for it.

Memories: A Small Cemetery in Virginia

I have a vague memory of my grandfather's taking me sometimes to a tiny chapel in the woods in tidewater Virginia.

This chapel was on the side of a remote, clayey hill, approachable from dirt roads off other dirt roads. It was always in danger of being overtaken by the ravenous pine forest surrounding it.

We went there only rarely, and in fact, nobody went there often. The chapel had long been abandoned as a church. Periodically, as I recall it, people with some connection to it gathered—maybe once a year—for what they called a "homecoming": an outdoor shared meal.

There was a brief service in the chapel, and then dinner. Older people visited, young folks showed off their babies, and kids ran around and played.

My grandfather was one of a few people who periodically spent a Saturday at the chapel doing whatever was needed. He cleared off encroaching weeds and brush, washed windows, made repairs, and always carefully tended the cemetery.

Kids seldom went into the cemetery. Many of the graves were very old—some dating into the 17th century, I believe.

Most of the headstones were smooth, illegible. Rain, wind, and temperature, the agents of time, had washed away their carvings long ago. Most of the stones had weakened and fallen beside the graves of people over whom they had loyally stood watch for as long as they could.

And all around that small clearing, the forest waited impatiently to obliterate any trace.

My grandfather's work, and the work of others who did as he did when they could, was to try to suspend time—to hold off the day when the chapel and cemetery finally succumbed to the forces of time and nature, and disappeared forever.

None of them had any connection to this chapel except that their families had been joined in its congregation generations ago. And that connection to the chapel was the only tie remaining among many of them.

They had full lives in different towns: families, friends and work to do. But some mysterious attachment held them to this remote, silent place and to the forgotten ancestors for whom it was sacred.

I think sometimes about those gravestones. We erect gravestones as tributes to memory, carving our names deeply into them. Some little inscriptions linking us to life, and some dates anchoring us in time.

But that information eventually slides from our memories, and those records slide from the stones and leach into the soil. All that remains is some little evidence that someone was there—and then that is swallowed up.

We survive only through those who come after us. The curve of a nose, the slope of a shoulder, a habit of thought—these lasting monuments are subtle, and mingled with those of others. But however subtle, something remains.

It may be a vague awareness shared among near-strangers that some place is important to them in a way they probably don't need to think much about.

I find this idea of immortality comfortable.

I know people who are happy to tell me exactly what will happen to me after I die. I have my doubts, though.

What feels right to me is the prospect of continuing in memory for as long as memory lasts, and eventually being reduced by time and reclaimed by nature.

In the long run the details of our existence—names, dates, achievements—don't matter much. What matters is that we were here briefly, and that the ripples we make on the surface of time will continue to spread, even as they lose their shape.

Desperately Seeking What's His Nickname

When I was young I wanted a good nickname. Unfortunately for me, my folks had deliberately given me a brief name, so there was little for anybody to work with.

If they had gone just one syllable further and called me, say, Robert, it would have worked. Bob. Rob. Bobby. Even Robin, I think, although this happens more in England than in Pitt County.

A nice long name would have worked even better. If my name were Alexander, I could have been Al, or Alex. How about Sandy?

They could have gone a little further yet and made a nickname mandatory. Aloysius, for instance: I would have been something like "Termite" before I cut my first tooth.

In the movies (we didn't have TV yet when this was an issue for me), all the really interesting kids had nicknames: "Stretch" for a tall kid, "Spanky" for a silly kid who gets into things, "Four-eyes" for the kid who wears glasses.

"Red" for you-know-who, although it was lost on us puerile patrons of black-and-white movies.

Now, where I lived we didn't actually use these exact nicknames. We didn't even turn Charles into Chuck. We made William into Bill or Billy, of course, and Peter into Pete. That doesn't take much doing.

One large friend whose name was Erwin was always addressed as "Sonny." This was a rule he would enforce, if necessary.

But our colorful nicknames were always unique and never, so far as I recall, referred to any visible physical feature.

Paul Cox

"Bump," for instance, for the son of a fellow who was, of course, called "Hump." Why was he called that? I have no idea: not to deride any physical deformity, because both father and son were actually quite handsome.

Why was a normal, ordinary grown man called "Pinky?" Why was a lucky kid called "Scut"? Who knows?

But I longed for such a distinction. Why couldn't people call me "Spike"? Maybe "The Flash"? Even "Scooter" would have been something.

How was I to get this nickname? I asked my mother, who suggested that if it were to be, it would be without my doing anything about it, and that I should get started on my homework. Big help.

I suppose it was all just a symptom of childhood. You spend your early years trying to figure out who you are and who you want to become.

You figure that a colorful, richly connotative nickname will help you establish an identity. Yeah, sure, I thought about it just like that: "richly connotative."

Anyway, I wanted to be a kid with a fascinating nickname. But it never happened.

Well, until later.

Of course, in college people addressed me with a number of quite richly connotative vulgarities, but that was just the times. Everybody called each other such things, but when they got down to cases, like whose turn is it to clean up this dump we live in, I was clearly and unambiguously "Paul."

So it went until my merry wife and I had kids.

Of course we gave them affectionate nicknames. I am forbidden by her stern injunction to tell you what we lovingly called our daughter. But "Benjamin" quickly became the "Banjo Man," shortened then to "Banjo." That was only within the household, however.

And they reciprocated with nicknames for us, as I have learned.

So now at last I have the nickname I have always wanted. But I'm not sure just what I want to do with it.

Does it give me the unique identity I was searching for?

Maybe "Dumbo" isn't really what I had in mind.

Why I Don't Like Going to Meetings

Many years ago my engaging wife got involved in many community issues. Fair housing, public school finance, the appropriate disposition of traffic signals. Stuff like that.

I thought that was pretty good. I appreciated that she should be kind of an activist, and tried to be supportive where I could. That is, I washed dishes on evenings when she went to Important Meetings.

But so infused did she become with civic-mindedness that she undertook to share her fun with me.

"You should get out and see what's going on in the community," she said. "Get involved. Go to meetings."

Now, I thought myself reasonably civic-minded: I paid my taxes cheerfully, aware that public services don't come free. I tried to keep up with the issues. I read about important happenings around me. I knew the Mayor's name.

But I didn't like going to meetings, and told my wife so.

"Nonsense," she explained. "You don't know what you're missing! Go to this meeting tonight! You'll enjoy it!" The meeting, she explained, had something to do with sanitation.

So after considerable cajoling, I agreed. This was back in the day when you wore a jacket and tie to public meetings, by the way, so it was no trivial commitment.

I drove toward the building where the meeting was to be. When I stopped for a traffic light, a complete stranger opened the door of my car and got in. Sat beside me and said, "OK, driver. Take me home."

I was uncertain what to do. I considered just driving to the police station, but thought that might have been a little transparent. I considered clubbing him with my free right hand, but didn't have much leverage. So I adopted an information strategy:

"Who are you?" I inquired.

The guy was instantly covered in confusion, alarm, dismay, contrition, and many other emotional states that are fun to spell. Mumbled that he had mistaken my car for his friend's, and was being clever. He blushed his way, muttering, out of the car and hurried off.

I gathered my composure and drove on to the meeting, where I received a greeting, a name tag, and a pin to fix it to my lapel with.

So I did, but I discovered too late that this was the one pin in a billion that had escaped milling. It was simply a straight, squared-off steel cylinder. Tore a ragged hole in my lapel. Ruined my jacket, made me look like a tramp.

I re-collected my composure and sat near the back of the meeting, which turned out to be a committee to organize a camping trip for Girl Scouts, and what job did I want to volunteer for.

"I thought this was about sanitation," I explained.

"Oh, wonderful! That's usually the hardest job to fill! Thank you so much!"

Getting out of this one took a while and a lot of stammering, smiling, and gesturing. I considered pretending to speak only Turkish, but remembered at the last moment that I had previously spoken when I rent my garment with the pin. Not in Turkish, either.

Somehow it seemed to me that my getting to the wrong meeting by mistake was cosmically connected with the guy getting into my car by mistake. We both looked and felt like idiots.

I thought of him, probably home by now, grinding his teeth in embarrassment; and I wondered whether I shouldn't find him, knock on his door, and offer to shake hands.

But I decided against that program, and went instead home to my wife.

Where we discussed my policy concerning meetings.

Taking Your Shot Best

About this time every year we all got shot.

That is to say, all the grade school students lined up by classes in the school corridors for what we called "tetnus [sic] shots." Whether they had anything to do with tetanus or not I don't know; that's just what we called them.

It was a grim business.

The corridors of our old school building were not the bright, pastel-painted hallways in schools now. Ours had oiled wooden floors and dark, grubby walls. Sounds reverberated in them eternally (it seemed), and some of the feeble overhead light globes were always out.

It was a grimy, dark place, like a dungeon, and we were a grimy set of whimpering, suffering kids. We supported the dungeon analogy.

Nobody was happy about these shots—well, nobody except for the occasional big kid who got a charge out of the misery of younger kids.

There were two nurses, from out of town, of course. They sat near the doors with big bowls of needles. Kids were shuffled past them, and each kid got a quick swab of alcohol, a stick, and another quick swab of alcohol.

It took about two or three seconds at most, and honestly, it didn't usually hurt much.

But the waiting in line took forever, and anticipation made the agony we expected pretty well unendurable.

It was, of course, a good test of machismo, although we didn't know that word back then.

As you progressed up through the grades, you were expected to endure the experience with increasing aplomb. The taller the line of kids, the dryer: that was, I think, the plan.

But there were always a few whose courage developed slower than others. Who, though they did their best, could not help yelping into tears when the stick finally stuck.

The nurse's reaction? "Go along, now."

All this anticipatory agony was stoked by excellent, gruesome rumors.

"They stuck this boy up in Ahoskie with too big of a needle? And it had a burr on the end? And his heart stopped! And he died right there!"

"Them nurses pretend to throw them needles away, but my cousin he seen one of them just dump them right back in the bowl when she thought nobody wasn't looking!"

"Some of that vaccine they use? Is POISON left over from the war! Spies snuck it in!"

"They stuck this boy in Tarboro with a bent needle, and it got caught in him! And they had to yank it out with pliers!"

Not that we ever witnessed any of this, you understand.

Of course, those who could manage it were expected to confirm their courage by saying something offhand and witty to the nurse as the needle plunged in. I think the nurses had heard it all, however, since they never reacted.

Anyway, eventually this slow torture, the price we had to pay for summer vacation, ended, and phase two began.

Phase two was what you did after the shot. The theory was that if you held your arm still, it would stiffen up. We were encouraged to pump our arms up and down for a few days.

All around town, then, you would see kids either flexing their arms like malfunctioning robots, or walking around looking kind of stiff and sore. Flexing was evidence that you knew what was what.

Pretty soon the shots were just a dim memory, and we embarked on the joys of summer in perfect form.

Our torment was past, and our robust health assured.

Ah, the good old days! They don't make corridors like that any more.

A January Night Scene

While driving down a country road in northeast Ohio one January night some years ago, I saw a sight that I hope to continue seeing as long as I live.

Although it was not late, the night was completely black. Northeast Ohio is a snowy area, owing to Lake Erie, and this night the road was just a black lane cut between snow banks about four feet high on both sides.

Moreover, it's an Amish area, so there were no power lines or telephone wires to interrupt the simple black-and-white of the scene. There was no moon that cloudy night, and no stars. There was nothing but me and my little white car, in an intensely cold dichromatic world.

As I drove along, I became aware of something ahead beside the road: a little twinkle of light bobbing along, and some glinting reflections near it.

As I got nearer, I saw that the light came from a kerosene lantern, held about knee-high by a tall man dressed in black, walking beside the road. Something he was carrying in his other hand reflected the light.

Then I saw that he wasn't alone. Beside him was a woman, also dressed in black, also carrying something in her hand that reflected the light.

As I continued, I saw more and more groups of these black-dressed people walking along the roadside with lanterns and strange, darkly shiny things swinging in their hands. Children tagged along behind many of them, all swinging the same burden.

I realized that these were Amish families, dressed as always in black or midnight blue. They were all going in the same direction, probably to the same place, carrying lanterns and the other mysterious things. Everyone seemed to walk lightly and fast, as if excited.

I slowed down to be certain that I didn't hit anyone in the narrow strip of road between the banks of snow.

Working among the Amish, I had learned to appreciate them.

The old-order Amish prefer a "plain" life—without electricity, tractors, cars, TV, or even buttons. They wear simple, dark clothing, live their old-fashioned way, and don't try to change others. They're decent, hard-working people, strict in their beliefs, genial with "Yankees," and always good neighbors.

After a while I rounded a turn in the road and saw a wonderful sight.

A pond beside the road was frozen hard. Around the pond a rough ring of kerosene lanterns suffused a steady bright light softly through the ice, so that the pond seemed to glow from within.

As they arrived, the Amish were sitting on logs and stones, strapping on ice skates—the odd glinting objects I had been wondering about.

Out on the ice several couples in solemn clothing glided around together in arcs and circles. Teenagers, with bare ankles above their skates, showed off. Little kids slipped and fell and tried again, some holding parents' hands.

I couldn't hear anything, shut in my car, but if I could have, I'm sure I would have heard laughter and fun. I had only a visual image of silent, dark, dignified people playing gracefully on the ice together, the whole scene haloed in a ring of bright gentle light.

To stop would have been to intrude, of course. I just drove slowly past and let this scene—severe and tender, grave and playful, calm and exhilarating, dark and brilliant—imprint itself on my mind.

And I continued through my night into another world altogether. One full of color and noise and electricity, but lacking, I realized, a splendid, humane magic that belongs to its own world.

Whistle While You. . .Whatever

Tell the truth, now: when an old Andy Griffith show rerun comes on, don't you whistle along with the theme music?

Sure you do. It's a pleasant tune, and besides, the professional whistler who recorded it was quite good.

Imagine that: a professional whistler.

A fellow I used to know was probably the greatest whistler in the world. Whistling wasn't his profession, however. He drove a garbage truck on which I worked.

When he wasn't whistling, Raymond (never Ray: he drove the truck) often sang, and he was a pretty competent crooner, too. But his whistling was what distinguished him.

Well, and his scientific understanding of garbage truck routes.

Raymond had a knack for redesigning his route so that he was able to finish up at least half an hour early each day. We hit every stop, did our work well, but somehow we finished our route early.

The supervisors used to expand our route just to fix Raymond, but somehow he could always redesign it to incorporate all the extra stops and still finish early.

The other route drivers therefore disliked him pretty intensely. I won't tell you his secret nickname, if you don't mind. Children might be nearby.

Anyway, all the experienced non-driving garbage men wanted to ride on Raymond's truck, partly because we finished early and partly because he maintained a cheerful atmosphere by his musical stylings.

Paul Cox

I was relatively inexperienced, but Raymond and I got along pretty well, so I managed to be on his truck most of the time.

Truth is, I was conspicuously slow at learning the routes, and sometimes got lost. I often wound up wandering the streets with 55 gallons of ripening garbage on my shoulder.

I think that my bewilderment may have contributed to the fun of our truck: people thought, correctly, that I had more determination than talent for the work. In other words, they got a kick out of my blunders.

But, ahem, we were talking about Raymond's whistling.

His whistling was modestly and tastefully ornamented, clear, and perfectly in tune. I don't think he was trying particularly to be artful about it, either. He was just talented.

As a whistler should be, he was even-tempered. He entertained the truck with music and occasionally told jokes. His route designs invariably took us past the Dairy Queen in mid-morning and some other such place in mid-afternoon, where we stopped for a little break.

By the way: if you're collecting garbage in 100-degree weather, don't buy a Slurpee and drink it fast. Take it from me.

Raymond would sit on a curb, drink coffee from a thermos, and chat with Doug, one of our regulars. I don't recall what they talked about, except that it was a peaceful kind of conversation, genial and companionable.

Then we got back on the truck and musically resumed our laborious haul through the city.

Maybe there's something about whistling—and singing to oneself—that goes along with a peaceful, philosophical disposition.

I doubt that whistling makes you carefree, but it may be a natural and inevitable expression of contentment with life. It's what we do because we can't wag our tails or purr.

Raymond, after all, was a pretty bright man in a profession that is not generally given much admiration.

There were some pretty unpleasant, sullen fellows on other trucks.

But here was a guy who seemed perfectly happy with himself, perfectly competent to control his circumstances. He was at ease with himself, and apparently unconcerned about jealous people around him.

What must professional whistlers be like, I wonder. What a life!

Never Give a Sucker—Period

You've heard the old admonition, "Never give a sucker an even break"?

The idea is that, once you have found someone gullible, then you should make it your project to take this person for all you can get.

It was a tough-guy sentiment a few years back when Americans thought it glamorous to be cynical, sharp, and a little unscrupulous.

But when I was a kid, and didn't know what an "even break" was, I found this sentence puzzling. It reminded me of "Spare the rod and spoil the child," which I thought was excellent advice. I used to remind my parents that it was considered wise.

I thought, in my innocence, that it really meant parents should spoil their children, not spank them, and I liked the sound of that. What did I know? I was something of a literal-minded kid.

But we were talking about giving suckers an even break. When I was a child, I thought this had something to do with giving suckers to people.

When my father took me to the barbershop, the barber, Mr. Nichols, would give me a sucker. He also parted my hair straight, which I suspected might be an "even break."

So I figured that this expression meant something about the way our culture instructed Mr. Nichols to treat the likes of me. Something about giving me a neat haircut and then a sucker.

I didn't have the syntax quite doped out—but when I was a kid it didn't bother me much to leave syntactical analysis until later. I overlooked the "never."

Other people gave me suckers too, as part of commercial transactions. The lady at the bank invited me to take a sucker when I appeared once a month with my teacher's paycheck and a deposit slip.

(Why did Miss Sealy let a third-grader deposit her paycheck? I dunno to this day, and I still don't really care. She was the teacher, and I did what she told me to do.) But we were talking about suckers.

Even the dentist gave me suckers. I never ate them, though, because I didn't care for this fellow, for some odd reason. (I've outgrown that.)

The truth is, I didn't much like suckers. Most of them were really more tart than I liked, and they lasted too long. I got bored with them. Who wants to labor all day over a tart chunk of hard candy, only to end up chewing a cud of fuzzy, wet paper?

But I thought that if an adult gave me some candy, I was expected to like it. The candy must be good, because the adult had endorsed it. So I dedicated many more days of my childhood than I liked to fooling with cheap suckers.

Nowadays I begin to see things more clearly.

I understand the reason why you seldom see adults pulling on suckers. They don't like them. People of discernment don't relish suckers.

Suckers aren't even designed, I expect, to be particularly tasty. They are not so much candy as little bribettes, given to children as tokens of good will. Something that says you can come back when your hair, in your parents' estimation, gets long.

I'm glad I've outgrown suckers. I mean by that that I'm glad to have gotten tall enough that merchants don't give them to me any longer. I find it a relief. At last I've been given an even break.

By the way, I won't tell you how I tumbled to the true meaning of "Spoil the rod and spare the child." That's a painful memory.

Report Card Day

Every six weeks, as I recall, came a special occasion: Report Card Day. To a kid, this was big stuff.

Report cards were yellow, crisply folded. Inside was a grid, with a column for each reporting period and a row for each subject.

I don't remember all the subjects, and they changed from year to year anyway. But it doesn't matter, because there were only a few basic grades. One was for reading and writing, one for arithmetic, and one for how much information you knew: history, geography, science, and the like.

These grades were important, to be sure, but only a little. We had some leeway.

The really important grade was at the bottom of the card: Conduct. One year they changed the word to "Deportment" but everybody knew it was really Conduct.

I've seen the language dressed up in other ways, too ("Works and plays well with others") but still—it's Conduct.

I don't know about you, but my mother made it clear that if I got a non-A on Conduct, I would have some sharp questions to answer.

Of course, there was a standard answer: "She's a mean old grouch who doesn't like me or anybody else and besides Jimmy really did it, not me, but she thought it was me, and I really didn't mean to do it, honest." Something like that.

The trouble with the Conduct grade was that it gave kids a difficult problem.

On the one hand, we were clearly expected to be somewhat mischievous. There were movies about The Little Rascals, not about The Little Good Kids. Dennis was a Menace, not a Pleasure (but on the TV show he was a goody-goody, and nobody liked it).

Huckleberry Finn and Tom Sawyer: think they got A's on Conduct?

Growing up to be somebody, we sensed, meant cultivating streaks and textures in your personality. "Bland" was no kind of personality to have—we instinctively knew we needed to seek out a way to be interesting people.

But being interesting could compromise your grade in Conduct. More interesting than about a B+ in Conduct was risky.

Too interesting, and you could be branded a "bad kid," and subjected to expectations no less difficult and no more appealing than those placed on a "good kid."

Of course, you had to live up (or down) to expectations.

The trick, then, was to be just interesting enough, but to know exactly where to draw the line so that your grade in Conduct wasn't a lightening rod.

Most years the State of North Carolina provided a little section on the back of the card where the teacher could write a brief note. Something like: "A delightful student," or "Has been working very hard." It was an elaboration on the Conduct grade, we all knew.

Need I say what my parents expected to see in this space?

Thus did our parents and teachers help to mold our little personalities. Thus they taught us that while they certainly wanted us to be competent students, what was bedrock essential is to be nice.

But not too nice. We had to find a spot for ourselves somewhere between tedious and vicious. The message of an A in Conduct was that that you hadn't gone off the deep end toward an impermissible level of interesting-ness.

I think that's about all I really learned in school. Well, punctuation and algebra, I suppose, and for some reason I still can name all the levels of the Linnaean system. But mostly I learned: no matter how smart or dumb I was, I'd better be nice.

Well, nice enough.

Memories of Finger Painting

It suddenly struck me the other day how much I miss finger-painting.

Not that I had a long career as a finger-painter. It lasted a couple of years when I was in elementary school, probably. Memory gives us vivid images from those years, but not much usable chronology.

And that's as it should be. I think that is how I experienced life back then—kind of unsystematically, without much planning or order.

Maybe that's why finger-painting was so much fun. Here was a nice rectangular piece of flat paper. It wasn't much like the world: it was squared off, orderly, perfectly clean, free of any character at all.

And here were messes of nice simple color. If you selected green, you got green. Not hunter green or fern green or springapple green—just green. Or blue, or red or yellow.

I never could see why anyone would want to finger-paint with yellow, but who cares? Nobody questioned my selection of blue, so I didn't care what others chose, either.

Now, a major issue of childhood is being messy. The standing order was, in general: don't.

Don't get messy. Don't leave your room messy. Comb your hair—it's messy. Don't play in your food, because that's messy. You remember.

So the idea that we could actually put our hands into the paint and then smear color all over this pristine surface was exciting. It was an audacious challenge to the code of our upbringing. It revealed that, while anti-messiness was indeed the general rule, there were exceptions. Sanctioned by teachers!

And when we got our hands all nice and slippery-drippy with the color, then we could paint anything we wanted! We were not constrained by any assignment—just paint whatever you like! Have fun!

So I started out with a circle. Parallel circumferences of fingertip tracks in a generic blue: looked great! A line through it! Some wavy lines below, like water maybe!

Squares, like houses! Squiggles that had no name, but looked really funny! Dots, which I made by just dabbing my fingertips onto the paper.

Oddly, we didn't get much paint on our clothes, or our knees or our faces.

Oh, I'm sure some kids must have, nature being what it is. Nowadays I might have expected the classroom to look like an explosion in a paint factory, but my actual recollection is that we somehow kept the mess within bounds. We were too absorbed in our art to worry about trying to get away with making a mess.

One year I painted a house. It was a box, of course, with a triangle on top and four stick people standing outside. A blue circle of sun in the sky, a tree that looked like blue broccoli beside the house. Our teacher admired it, and hung it—with 22 others—on the wall.

Next year I painted a bridge over a ravine. There was a river running at the bottom of the ravine, and the bridge seemed to teeter above. It was dramatic and exciting.

But then I thought: this is kind of experimental. Maybe people won't get it. I had had pretty good luck with the house last year.

So I retreated to safety. I wiped away the bridge and painted another house, like before. My new teacher looked at it, and seemed disappointed.

"What happened to the bridge?" she asked. I didn't have much of an answer, but I realized I had made an artistic mistake.

I think that was pretty much when I lost interest in finger-painting. Too easy: you never knew when you were right.

A Critique of Perfectly Good Reason

When she was quite young, my sister loved dinner rolls. Generally they were those brown-'n'-serve kind, which always taste better than you expect them to.

Once in the early stages of a meal—I think it was the part just after "Amen"—my sister quickly took and ate a couple of rolls, just to be certain she wouldn't get shorted.

My mother, appropriately horrified, cried out: "Jane! You mustn't just push rolls into your mouth like that!"

To which my sister, smiling, replied: "Well, I can't pull them in."

Normally such cheek would have put her in the way of an early bedtime, but my mother was so diverted by her drollery that she let it go, and I believe she did the right thing.

Some people are blessed to see things a little differently.

I knew a fellow in college who insisted on cutting his own hair. He had money enough to go to a barber, but preferred to cut it himself.

Now, through practice, standing in front of a mirror, he had gotten to where he did pretty well in the front. But in back, he just kind of guessed at where the longer hair might be found. So his haircuts, starting at about the ears, were just random chopping: a hole here, a tuft there.

I once asked him: "Grady, why do you do that? The back of your head looks like a chicken yard. Is that really what you want?"

"Oh, I don't care about that," he said. "I'm never back there."

"But what about other people who see you from behind?"

"Their problem, I guess."

Or there's the person who asked the Department of Transportation to take away the DEER CROSSING sign near his house. Said he thought the sign was a bad idea, because too often when the deer crossed there, they got run over. You probably read about this on the Internet.

Or the lady who wondered why traffic lights should have buzzers that sounded for red. Somebody explained that those were for the blind. She was aghast: "What are blind people doing driving?"

Or the airlines clerk who asks you whether anyone has tampered with your baggage without your knowing it.

It doesn't take much to turn sense upside down. Just a word here or there, and suddenly you realize that we don't all live in exactly the same world, and that some of those worlds are dumber—and some much less dumb—than the one we thought was standard.

I once had a guy explain to me why I should pay for a refrigerator purchased by someone else in another state with my name. He said that even though I hadn't exactly bought the refrigerator, I got the benefit of the good credit rating that had enabled the other Paul Cox to buy it, and I should be grateful for that and try to protect it. (I demurred, by the way.)

Finally, to return to my sister. I recall once when she was quite young, she had some hot chocolate. Too hot, in fact.

My brother and I, being older, naturally had the responsibility of leading our sister into trouble or distress whenever we could. So we encouraged her to take a big chug of the screaming hot chocolate.

Nope, she said. She was waiting for it to get warm.

"Warm? Don't you mean you're waiting for it to get cool?"

"No, dummy," she explained. "I don't want to drink it cool. I want to drink it warm."

See what I mean? How can you reason with a person like that?

The Art of Analogy

It's a little like....

When my sister was very young—3 or 4, I think—she didn't understand the idea of analogy. She appeared not to have noticed that the two things being compared needed to have something important in common.

She might say she was "so tired as a nail" or that something was "so sharp as a cantaloupe." (She always said "so" rather than "as.")

Well, my sister was a brilliant child then and is a brilliant woman now. So it may be that in her head she found common ground between fatigue and nails, or between sharpness and cantaloupes.

Nobody else could, though, so her analogies usually left us looking puzzled.

The trouble with analogy is that so many of the really good ones have been taken already.

If I say someone is "as mad as a wet hen," you won't care very much. You won't think about it at all, because you first heard this analogy years ago. You thought about it then, liked it, got used to it. So much so that now it doesn't register with you at all. Doesn't make you think about being angry, or about wet hens. You just hear it and don't notice.

Like "as sharp as a tack," or "as slow as molasses." Why bother with such analogies, if they don't provoke the hearer or reader to think about sharpness or slowness?

So thinking of a fresh analogy—one that will give you a new understanding of something—is difficult.

Let's try one: As quick as—as what? Maybe "as quick as a paper cut"? That may work. How about another: "as big as a hole in a tooth." Like that one? You can have these for free, but after a few uses, they too will be old and worn out.

Some comedy writers try to characterize rural people by having them use particularly colorful analogies. But the analogies writers invent for them seem artificial and clumsy.

"As nervous as a long-tailed cat in a roomful of rocking chairs," for instance, is a good idea, but it's too long. Most of us check out by the time the word "roomful" comes along. And some of the analogies get just ridiculous. "As pretty as a june bug on the brim of Sally Mae's flowered hat." See what I mean? Too long, too complicated, too cornball. Overdone.

We don't hear many really good new analogies. They're hard to think of, and we get used to thinking of our world in the same old way day in and day out.

Maybe that's why I remember my baby sister's analogies. When she said, on a sunny summer afternoon, "Whew! I'm so hot as an egg!" she made me think. How hot must she be? Aren't eggs really kind of cool? But a boiled egg is damp inside, like a sweating person. And I guess when you boil them. . . .

And soon I had a pretty good idea of just how hot my little sister felt.

"This watermelon," she might say, "is so good as a dime!" For all its obscurity, it gave me a good idea just how good the watermelon really was. Of course, that was back when a dime was better than it is now. And so was a watermelon, come to think of it.

If the purpose of analogy is to give the hearer an insight into the mind of the speaker, and my little sister's mind was kind of unusual, then I guess her analogies worked pretty well.

Yes sir. Her analogies were so clever as soap.

Storms of All Kinds

We were talking after dinner the other night, and the subject of storms came up.

Everyone has a story to tell about a storm. Generally they involve the line that separates adventure from fear.

I've told the one about the walnut tree that got hit by lightening right above our house one night. The house had a tin roof, and the tree was bearing walnuts, so it was a memorable experience.

And I have watched thunderstorms gather across Chicago, turn the sky green, and illuminate the city with heroic bursts of light. The city would be bathed in terrifying power for a while, and emerge fresh and clean.

There's something about storms that satisfies us deeply. They reach 'way down inside us and make us feel right. Refreshed, shook down, cleansed.

I suppose one way to think about life is that it is a constant cycle of gathering force and releasing force. Tensions build up in our lives, and we release them if we can. Maybe with laughter, maybe with squabbles, maybe with intense work; but once the tensions are released we feel relieved and perhaps well used.

Perhaps that's why we like thunderstorms. They replicate in the heavens the kind of massive shudder that periodically makes things all right again.

When I was very little, my brother and I used to visit my grandparents in a small town in Virginia. They lived across the street from the Baptist Church to which my Grandmother belonged. (Granddaddy was a Methodist, but that's another story.)

Paul Cox

On Wednesday evenings we sat on the front porch in the swing with Granddaddy while our Grandmother attended Prayer Meeting across the street. We could hear the quiet sounds of the hymns they sang, songs like "Sweet Hour of Prayer," and "The Lord is My Shepherd."

Meanwhile off in the distance, across the river, it seemed, a summer storm usually blew up. We would hear little rumblings of thunder, and some polite lightening would pulse through the dark sky far away from us.

We rocked on the swing and chatted quietly with the neighbors, who speculated on whether we would get any rain from this storm. The consensus was generally that we might.

Eventually the Prayer Meeting would break up, and people would emerge from the church, stopping to visit on the steps, laughing together, planning to get together for supper next week, telling about kids and grandkids.

A few of the members would drift across the street to us on the porch, where they would stop for a few minutes to chat with my Granddaddy.

"See you've got the grandchildren with you, Mr. Chandler."

"Oh, yes. They're here for a few days."

"You boys treating your Granddaddy pretty well, now, aren't you?"

"Yes sir, trying to."

The conversation was always the same—quiet, polite, friendly, easy. We rocked quietly on the swing and completed this conversation several times through the evening. Then my Grandmother joined us and the adults would talk quietly as the exhausted thunderstorm across the river wandered off muttering and growling, as if looking for something.

The conversation got more and more distant, the voices more and more faint; and then miraculously my brother and I would awaken in our beds to a whole new morning.

It was a gentle, peaceful way to wrap up gentle, peaceful days. It was a warm, quiet world of good people, soft storms, security, and sweet, vague memories—mild hymns, faint lightening, faraway music, and rocking with Granddaddy on the porch.

Everybody has at least one storm story. I have several, and I feel pretty lucky to have them.

About the Author

Paul Cox is a father and grandfather, a brother, a husband and a southerner who loves eastern North Carolina barbecue, words, and cornbread. He retired in 1998 from careers in which he taught 17th century British literature, served as a university administrator, engineered software, and consulted on Y2K issues. In retirement he took up writing newspaper columns for *The Transylvania Times* (Brevard, North Carolina), and in 2001 won the first place award for humorous columns in the annual North Carolina Press Association competition. With his emphatic wife Susan and two chronically drowsy but funny cats, he now lives, reads and plays chess among the mountains and waterfalls of western North Carolina, and considers himself pretty lucky.

Printed in the United States
21536LVS00003B/52